THE TRUE DEVOTION TO THE BLESSED VIRGIN

Treatise on The True Devotion to the Blessed Virgin

by

SAINT LOUIS–MARIE DE MONTFORT

BARONIUS PRESS
MMXI

First published in 2006 by
Baronius Press Ltd
London · United Kingdom · www.baroniuspress.com

© Baronius Press Limited, 2006.
This edition 2011.

11 10 9 8 7 6 5 4
ISBN (13 digit): 978-1-905574-30-8   Paperback

This edition has been re-typeset using the text of the 1947 edition originally published by The Fathers of the Company of Mary, Colbury, Totton under the imprimatur of Johannes Henricus, Epus Portus Magni, 21st May 1947.

Paperback Cover Picture: An artist's impression of *The Virgin and Child* by William Bouguereau.

Printed in India

CONTENTS

CHAPTER ONE
NECESSITY OF DEVOTION TO THE BLESSED VIRGIN

CHAPTER TWO
FUNDAMENTAL TRUTHS CONCERNING DEVOTION TO OUR BLESSED LADY.

CHAPTER FOUR

NATURE OF THE PERFECT DEVOTION TO THE BLESSED VIRGIN, or THE PERFECT CON-SECRATION TO JESUS CHRIST

CHAPTER FIVE

THE MOTIVES WHICH RECOMMEND THIS DEVOTION TO US

CHAPTER SIX

BIBLICAL FIGURE OF THIS PERFECT DEVOTION: REBECCA AND JACOB

CHAPTER SEVEN

THE WONDROUS EFFECTS WHICH THIS DEVOTION PRODUCES IN A SOUL THAT IS FAITHFUL TO IT.

CHAPTER EIGHT
SPECIAL PRACTICES OF THIS DEVOTION.

SUPPLEMENT
HOW TO PRACTISE THIS DEVOTION IN HOLY COMMUNION

Preface to this Edition

The True Devotion to the Blessed Virgin is probably, with St Alphonsus Liguori's *The Glories of Mary*, the most celebrated and highly regarded treatise ever written on Our Lady. Unpublished during the life of the saint, it has enjoyed the vigorous endorsement of the many outstanding popes the Church has been blessed with since its discovery in 1842; and, although it went into something of an eclipse in the irresponsible ecumenical frenzy which followed Vatican II (Mary being a stumbling block for Protestants), John Paul II was to prove an eloquent champion, crediting *True Devotion* with a turning-point in his spiritual life, adopting his motto, *Totus tuus*, from St. Louis, and admitting him to the Universal Calendar. So we can see that there has been something of a de Montfort revival of late. Nevertheless, it would be true to say that St. Louis has always been rather less appreciated, and even less known, than we should expect of a missionary, mystic and theologian of his stature. I suspect that this is not an accident, but rather mysteriously consistent with the hidden efficacy of his influence during his lifetime.

Louis Marie Grignon de la Bacheleraie was born at Montfort on 31 January, 1673. When he was twelve, he was sent to the Jesuit college at Rennes. At the age of nineteen, he decided to pursue his studies in Paris (at St. Sulpice), making the long journey on foot, and giving away all his money to the poor on the way. Ordained priest at twenty-seven, he found his true vocation as a missionary to his native Brittany and the neighbouring Vendée five years later. A magnificent orator and catechist, and a transparently holy man, he worked a revolution in the religious life of the locals. For this, he earned the unforgiving hostility of the Jansenists. The Catholic Encyclopaedia recounts the most famous episode of this contest:

Grignion's extraordinary influence was especially apparent in the matter of the calvary at Pontchateau. When he announced his determination of building a monumental calvary on a neighbouring hill, the idea was enthusiastically received by the inhabitants. For fifteen months between two and four hundred peasants worked daily without recompense, and the task had just been completed, when the king commanded that the whole should be demolished, and the land restored to its former condition. The Jansenists had convinced the Governor of Brittany that a fortress capable of affording aid to persons in revolt was being erected, and for several months five hundred peasants, watched by a company of soldiers, were compelled to carry out the work of destruction. Father de Montfort was not disturbed on receiving this humiliating news, exclaiming only: "Blessed be God!"

St. Louis' trust in God was amply vindicated, for not only was the calvary eventually rebuilt, but his mission territories – Brittany and the Vendée – were the only parts of France to resist the Revolution seventy-five years after his death, remaining Catholic strongholds well into the late twentieth century: St. Louis had done his work well.

The same is true of the two congregations St. Louis founded shortly before his death – the Sisters of Wisdom (devoted to hospital work and the instruction of poor girls), and the Company of Mary (missionaries). At his death, these congregations numbered respectively only four sisters and two priests with a few brothers: both were to grow into major congregations whose activities stretched across the globe.

And so we find the same pattern with *True Devotion*: it seems appropriate that his most famous book was unpublished in his lifetime. As for the contents of this work of spiritual genius, it is enough to point out here that the key to de Montfort's Marian spirituality is that he considered Our Lady to be the infallible and chosen gate to the heart of Christ – To Jesus through Mary: it is Christ Himself Who is at the centre of *True Devotion*.

St. Louis Grignon de Montfort died at St. Laurent-sur-Sèvre, 28 April, 1716. He was beatified by Leo XIII in 1888, and canonized by Pius XII in 1947.

Robert Asch

Father Faber's Preface

It was in the year 1846 or 1847, at St. Wilfrid's, that I first studied the life and spirit of the Venerable Grignion de Montfort; and now, after more than fifteen years, it may be allowable to say that those who take him for their master will hardly be able to name a Saint or ascetical writer, to whose grace and spirit their mind will be more subject than to his. We may not yet call him Saint; but the process of his beatification is so far and so favourably advanced that we may not have long to wait before he will be raised upon the altars of the Church.

There are few men in the eighteenth century who have more strongly upon them the marks of the man of Providence than this Elias like missionary of the Holy Ghost and of Mary. His entire life was such an exhibition of the holy folly of the Cross, that his biographers unite in always classing him with St Simon Salo and St Philip Neri. Clement XI made him a missionary apostolic in France, in order that he might spend his life in fighting against Jansenism, so far as it affected the salvation of souls. Since the apostolical epistles it would be hard to find words that burn so marvellously as the twelve pages of his prayer for the Missionaries of the Holy Ghost, to which I earnestly refer all those who find it hard to keep up under their numberless trials the first fires of the love of souls. He was at once persecuted and venerated everywhere. His amount of work, like that of St Anthony of Padua, is incredible and, indeed, inexplicable. He wrote some spiritual treatises, which have already had a remarkable influence on the Church during the few years they have been known, and bid fair to have a much wider influence in years to come. His preaching, his writing, and his conversation were all impregnated with prophecy and with anticipations of the later ages of the Church. He comes forward like another St Vincent Ferrer, as if on the days bordering on the Last Judgment, and proclaims that he brings an authentic message from God about the greater honour and wider knowledge and more prominent love of His Blessed Mother, and her connection with the second advent of her Son. He founded two religious congregations—one of men and one of women—which have been quite extraordinarily successful; and yet he died at the age of forty-three in 1716, after only sixteen years of priesthood.

It was on the 12th of May, 1853, that the decree was pronounced at Rome, declaring his writing to be exempt from all error which could be a bar to his canonisation. In this very treatise on the veritable devotion to Our Blessed Lady, he has recorded this prophecy: "I clearly foresee that raging brutes will come in fury to tear with their diabolical teeth this little writing and him whom the Holy Ghost has made use of to write it; or at least to envelop it in the silence of a coffer, in order that it may not appear." Nevertheless, he prophesies both its appearance and its success. All this was fulfilled to the letter. The author died in 1716, and the treatise was found by accident by one of the priests of his congregation at St Laurent-sur-Sèvre in 1842. The existing Superior was able to attest the handwriting as being that of the venerable founder; and the autograph was sent to Rome to be examined in the process of canonisation.

All those who are likely to read this book love God; and lament that they do not love Him more; all desire something for His glory—the spread of some good work, the success of some devotion, the coming of some good time. One man has been striving for years to overcome a particular fault, and has not succeeded. Another mourns, and almost wonders while he mourns, that so few of his relations and friends have been converted to the faith. One grieves that he has not devotion

enough; another that he has a cross to carry, which is a pe-
culiarly impossible cross to him; while a third has domestic
troubles and family unhappinesses, which feel almost incom-
patible with his salvation; and for all these things prayer appears to bring so little remedy. But what is the remedy that
is wanted? what is the remedy indicated by God Himself? If
we may rely on the disclosures of the Saints, it is an immense
increase of devotion to Our Blessed Lady; but, remember,
nothing short of an *immense* one. Here, in England, Mary is
not half enough preached. Devotion to her is low and thin
and poor. It is frightened out of its wits by the sneers of heresy. It is always invoking human respect and carnal prudence,
wishing to make Mary so little of a Mary that Protestants
may feel at ease about her. Its ignorance of theology makes it
unsubstantial and unworthy. It is not the prominent characteristic of our religion which it ought to be. It has no faith in
itself. Hence it is that Jesus is not loved, that heretics are not
converted, that the Church is not exalted; that souls, which
might be saints, wither and dwindle; that the Sacraments are
not rightly frequented, or souls enthusiastically evangelised.
Jesus is obscured because Mary is kept in the background.
Thousands of souls perish because Mary is withheld from
them. It is the miserable unworthy shadow which we call our
devotion to the Blessed Virgin that is the cause of all these
wants and blights, these evils and omissions and declines. Yet,
if we are to believe the revelations of the Saints, God is *pressing* for a greater, a wider, a stronger, quite another devotion
to His Blessed Mother. I cannot think of a higher work or
a broader vocation for anyone than the simple spreading of
this peculiar devotion of the Venerable Grignion de Montfort. Let a man but try it for himself, and his surprise at the
graces it brings with it, and the transformations it causes in
his soul, will soon convince him of its otherwise almost in-

credible efficacy as a means for the salvation of men, and for the coming of the kingdom of Christ. O, if Mary were but known, there would be no coldness to Jesus then! O, if Mary were but known, how much more wonderful would be our faith, and how different would our Communions be! O, if Mary were but known, how much happier, how much holier, how much less worldly should we be, and how much more should we be living images of our sole Lord and Saviour, her dearest and most Blessed Son!

I have translated the whole treatise myself, and have taken great pains with it, and have been scrupulously faithful. At the same time, I would venture to warn the reader that one perusal will be very far from making him master of it. If I may dare to say so, there is a growing feeling of something inspired and supernatural about it, as we go on studying it; and with that we cannot help experiencing, after repeated readings of it, that its novelty never seems to wear off, nor its fulness to be diminished, nor the fresh fragrance and sensible fire of its unction ever to abate. May the Holy Ghost, the Divine Zealot of Jesus and Mary, deign to give a new blessing to this work in England; and may He please to console us quickly with the canonisation of this new apostle and fiery missionary of His most dear and most Immaculate Spouse; and still more with the speedy coming of that great age of the Church, which is to be the Age of Mary!

F. W. FABER
Priest of the Oratory

Presentation of Our Blessed Lady, 1862.

Letter to the Clergy, Secular and Regular, of the Diocese of Salford

By HERBERT VAUGHAN, *at that time Bishop of Salford, afterwards Cardinal-Archbishop of Westminster.*

Very Rev. and Rev. Dear Fathers and Brethren in Jesus Christ,—The sanctification of the soul is more dependent upon Our Blessed Lady's continuous care and maternal love than upon the influence of any other creature. As the Incarnation of God depended upon her goodwill and consent, so the elevation of man to a state of eternal beatitude depends upon her assistance. Mary is no less necessary to the redeemed than she was to the Redeemer; and theology tells us that she was necessary to Him by a necessity called hypothetical.

Constituted as we are, by our office, guide of men along the rugged path of life, we are doubly bound to make a special study of Mary's place in the work of man's sanctification. It is not enough to recognise her singular prerogatives; we must proclaim and explain them, until men know her, love her, and fly to her, as to the *Felix cœli Porta*.

This, then, is one reason for causing to be published and dedicating to you, dear Rev. Fathers and Brethren, this third edition of the Venerable Grignion de Montfort's *Treatise on the True Devotion to the Blessed Virgin*. Another reason is, that this little work seems to have a quite unspeakable value for any one who has a pronounced consecration of himself to the Blessed Virgin, and through her to God.

Many of us have happily been brought up by pious parents, who instilled a tender devotion to the Blessed Virgin into our hearts from the dawn of reason. Many of us were led later on, by pious masters or confessors, to make a solemn consecration of ourselves to this good Mother. We well remember the grave moment when we publicly made this religious consecration of ourselves to her in the Sodality Chapel at Stonyhurst, now forty years ago. To consecrate oneself to her is an instinct of Catholic faith, and a practice very widely spread among the Catholic laity in England, as well as among the clergy.

Some acts of devotion are transient—if we may call any supernatural act transient, whose fragrance and bloom are imperishable, and destined to enter into the sum of our joy for eternity, while others ought to be permanently energising within us, strengthening and deepening in our soul through life. Such, for instance, are the vows made in baptism, the vows of our priesthood, our apostolic vow to serve the mission, our religious vows if we have any, and such also is our solemn consecration to the Blessed Mother of God. The vows of baptism we understood nothing of, at the time we made them; our Consecration to Mary was probably appreciated only according to the mind of a child, its full significance being veiled under a very imperfect knowledge. The first was not a mere ceremony, the second was not a passing sentiment of devotion. Each was intended, in its separate way, to be a life-long reality.

The Catechism of the Council of Trent exhorts parish priests to teach their people the meaning of their baptismal vows; and their solemn renewal is not infrequently repeated in our churches, at the close of missions and retreats.

A quite extraordinary spiritual benefit to the whole soul may also be derived from a careful study and realisation of the consecration we once made of ourselves to the Blessed Virgin. Indeed, such a study is necessary if the consecration is to last, and if the soul is to bear its proper consecrated fruit. The reason why so much piety is shallow and evanescent, why religion so frequently fails to take hold of the mind, and to govern the conduct of the stronger natures, is because the intellect has not been thoroughly engaged on the side of religion. The more intellect is developed by education, the more it must be pressed into the service of God.

Now, De Montfort's *Treatise on True Devotion to the Blessed Virgin* appeals as strongly to the intellect as it does to the heart. Any one who has really mastered it will feel that his consecration to Mary has been sensibly raised to a higher plane, and flooded with new light. He will also see its close and important connection with the renewal of his baptismal vows.

I remember reading it when Father Faber published his English translation of it in 1862, not long before his own death. And I well remember how enthusiastically Monsignor Newsham, the venerable and beloved President of Ushaw College, wrote about it and recommended it in all directions. I had not read it again till last summer, when it fell in my way apparently by accident. I then gave a whole week to the constant and exclusive study of it, and have been frequently reading it ever since. One result of this study has been a full realisation of Father Faber's words: "I would venture to warn the reader of this Treatise"—these are his words—"that one perusal will be very far from making him a master of it … after repeated readings of it, its novelty never seems to wear off, nor its fulness to be diminished, nor the fresh fragrance and sensible fire of its unction ever to abate." And another result was a determination to get it reprinted, in order that I might place a copy of it in the hands of every priest in the diocese, with a counsel not to be satisfied, as I had been twenty years ago, with one perusal of it, but to read it repeatedly, so as to experience personally the transformation it is capable of working in the soul.

There are expressions in this Treatise that may sound strange to ears educated in the cold, critical, controversial atmosphere of England, where even good people have sometimes felt apologetically in admitting the sovereignty and sway of their heavenly Queen. Heresy, on the absurd and pharisaical pretence of zeal for God, chides and condemns that generous and unrestrained outpouring of confidence and affection for the Mother of their Redemption, the Mother of their Sanctification and Salvation, which is so natural to the children of Mary, and which gives them a Christ-like character. It has consequently had much to say against this Treatise. I may, therefore, observe that the process for De Montfort's canonisation is far advanced. His virtues have been declared to have been heroic, and all his writings free from anything contrary to faith or morals, or to the Church's common sentiment or practice. The Congregation of Rites has now passed to the examination of the miracles. His writings are, therefore, in the same category as the works of St Alphonso, which no one may condemn as unsound, though we are free to discuss their merits or lay them aside, if we find they do not suit or help us. The teaching of De Montfort was very closely examined some years ago by a learned theologian, in the first volume of the *Analecta Pontificia,* and again, in the preface to the English edition of his life. Dr. Pusey attacked it in his *Eirenicon,* and thus gave to Dr. Ward an opportunity of defending it in a most masterly way in the *Dublin Review.* The series of articles then put forth have since been published in a single volume, entitled *Essays, Devotional and Scriptural.*

I will notice only one objection that may be raised against De Montfort's doctrine: namely, that it interferes with that straight and direct intercourse with the Sacred Humanity which is our greatest honour and privilege: and that, it sets *her* pattern before us for imitation rather than that of Our Blessed Lord. The objection is more specious than real. Of course, Our Blessed Lord is "the Way, the Truth, and the Life" for each one of us, and He Himself has said, "Come ye all to *Me.*" But surely we go none the less straight, none the less securely to the Son, because we beseech His Mother to take us by the hand, and to accompany us, and to put in a motherly word for her poor children. It is most reasonable to suppose that we shall find Him the more quickly and the more certainly if we approach Him by the very path which He Himself trod in coming to us—no other than the path of His Blessed Mother.

If our Guardian Angel mercifully attends us in every step we make and never leaves us absolutely alone, what difficulty can there be in beseeching Mary never to leave us for a moment and to show us more and more clearly on each occasion the blessed fruit of her womb?

If even Satan be sometimes allowed to possess the souls and bodies of men for an evil purpose or for their mysterious trial, may we not believe that Mary, who carried the whole mystical body of Christ within her heart, possesses at least an equal power over our souls and bodies—for our welfare and happiness?

But, in truth, the whole doctrine of this Venerable Apostle of Mary is little more than an expansion of those beautiful and pregnant words of the liturgical hymn:

"Monstra te esse Matrem.

Sumat per te preces,

Qui pro nobis natus

Tulit esse tuus."

Though one of De Montfort's counsels, which of course we are free to adopt or not as we please, goes so far as to recommend an *explicit* reference to Mary in all our prayers, so as never to separate Jesus and Mary in our thoughts, he says that this can be done by a mere glance of the mind towards Mary, and that it need in no way hinder the mind in its contemplation of the Sacred Humanity.

And if, as he says, the best way to imitate Jesus is to imitate His Blessed Mother, what is this but to act upon a principle again and again inculcated by the Holy Spirit Himself in the New Testament?[1] "*Rogo ego vos, imitatores mei estote, sicut et ego Christi,*" says St Paul to the Corinthians. "*Et vos imitatores nostri facti, et Domini,*" he writes to the Thessalonians.[2] "*Imitatores mei estote fratres, et observate eos qui ita ambulant sicut habetis formam nostram*"—so you have "our model"—is the injunction he presses upon the Philippians.[3] Here, then, the principle is clearly laid down, the Venerable Grignion applied it, like St Ambrose, who wrote, "Let the soul of Mary be in each of us to magnify the Lord; let the spirit of Mary be in each of us to rejoice in God."

But there can be no mistake as to the teaching of De Montfort, and its direct tendency to bring us into union with Jesus Christ. This is worth insisting on by one or two quotations from his words: "I avow with all the Church, that Mary, being but a mere creature that has come from the hands of the Most High, is, in comparison with His Infinite Majesty, less than an atom, or rather, she is nothing at all." Again, "the predestinate well know what is the most sure, the most easy, the most short, and the most perfect means by which *to go to Jesus Christ:* and they will deliver themselves to Mary, body and soul without reserve, *that they may thus be all for Jesus Christ.*" "Jesus Christ our Saviour, true God and true Man, ought to be the last end of all our other devotions, *else they are false and delusive.*" And again, "If we establish the solid devotion to Our Blessed Lady, *it is only to establish more perfectly the devotion to Jesus Christ,* and to put forward an easy and secure means for finding Jesus Christ. *If devotion to Our Lady removed us from Jesus Christ, we should have to reject it as an illusion of the devil.*"

---

1 1 Cor. iv, 16.
2 Thes. i, 6.
3 Phil. iii, 17.

Like some of the Saints, the Venerable Grignion de Mont-fort seems to have been charged by God with a special mission. He declares that he comes with a distinct message, and he speaks like one inspired by the gift of prophecy. Two hundred years ago he spoke of a marvellous increase of devotion to Mary then to come; he declared that devotion to Mary will make the great Saints that are to appear at the end of the world. He asserted positively that "God wishes that His holy Mother should be more known, more loved, more honoured, than she has ever been," and "that the Most High with His holy Mother has to form for Himself great Saints who shall surpass most of the other Saints in sanctity as much as the cedars of Lebanon outgrow the little shrubs."

Part of his prophecy has been already fulfilled, as all can see. I say nothing of his prophecy as to what should befall his Treatise on Devotion to Our Lady, and of how strangely it has been verified; but I cannot help pointing out the fact that a number of Festivals in honour of Our Lady have been instituted since De Montfort's death in 1716, and that religious Congregations of both sexes have been established, almost without number, either under the name of Mary, or in honour of her prerogatives and the mysteries connected with her life. With what marvellous zeal, too, the Bishops and people of the whole of Christendom petitioned Pius IX to define her Immaculate Conception, and with what solemnity and rejoicings was it not at last defined! And now the successor of Pius IX, a Pontiff whose characteristic is learning, and whose Apostolic Letters are addressed especially to the intellect of the age, has thrown himself and the whole Church upon the bosom of Mary with a devotion and faith never surpassed. Leo XIII commanded and decreed a thing never before heard of: that the Rosary and the Litany of Mary should be sung or recited in every church, where there is charge of souls, throughout the world, and that not once or twice, but for a period of time exceeding a month. Surely all this is after the spirit and prediction of De Montfort. And still further, as though to point out the most intimate personal relationship still existing between Mary and Jesus and the importance of invoking both together, the Holy Father commanded that her Rosary and Litany should be recited either in connection with the Holy Sacrifice of the Mass, or at Exposition and Benediction of the Blessed Sacrament. Assuredly the increase of devotion to Mary during the last two hundred years has been quite extraordinary and unprecedented. Nor was there anything two centuries ago, when everything appeared so dark, to warrant this marvellous growth. If one part of the prophecy of De Montfort has been verified under our own eyes, we are naturally led to believe that he spoke by the Spirit of God, and that the remaining part, referring to the latter days, may yet be fulfilled. And thus we are again drawn by a number of further considerations to do all we can, as pastors of souls, to deepen devotion to Mary, and to perfect that consecration to her which we ourselves and our penitents may have made in years gone by, "in order that thus," in the words of De Montfort, "we may be all for Jesus Christ."

Finally, while the Vicar of Christ has turned the whole mind and heart of the Church to Mary, we may be certain that the Heavenly Patron of the Universal Church has been watching over the Pontiff and the people of God. He of all the Saints is best able to teach us how to think of Mary, how to honour her. As St Teresa said, "If you know not how to pray, take Joseph for your master, and you will not go astray." St Joseph necessarily leads the members of the mystical body of Christ to the love of their Mother, his own most blessed Spouse. He will have part and lot with her and with the Church during those latter ages of the world when the struggle between good and evil shall become intensified. He well knows that *she* will finally destroy all heresies, that *she* will finally and for ever crush with her heel the serpent's head. He will, therefore, help us to perfect our consecration, to Mary. As Joseph and Mary shared the humiliation and obscurity of the Redeemer for thirty years, they will take a conspicuous and noble part with Him in the glory and triumph of the Church at the end of the world.

Meanwhile, may Mary often communicate with your souls, not, indeed, after the manner of those who are in the flesh, but by those intellectual operations which are proper, St Thomas tells us, to the Blessed; operations which are not hindered by local distance, and which often take place in the kingdom of the soul, even without our knowledge or consciousness.

May the constant use of her Rosary multiply your joy in conversions; and may the frequent perusal of this Treatise so illumine your soul with the clear and blessed light of this most sweet "Morning Star," as to enable you to lead innumerable souls by a most natural and easy way into the burning and all-absorbing love of "Jesus, the Son of Justice."

Wishing you every grace and blessing,

I am, always,

Very Rev. and Rev. dear Fathers,

Your faithful and devoted Servant,

✠ HERBERT,

Bishop of Salford.

Bishop's House, Salford,
Nov. 1, 1883.

Introduction

1. It is through the most Blessed Virgin Mary that Jesus Christ came into the world, and it is through her that He must reign in the world.

2. Mary was most hidden during her life: for this reason she is called by the Holy Ghost and the Church *Alma Mater*[1] "Mother hidden and secret." So profound was her humility that her strongest and most constant inclination on earth was to remain hidden from herself and from all creatures in order to be known to *God Alone.*

3. In answer to the prayers which she made to be hidden, poor and humble, God was pleased to conceal her from nearly every other human creature in her conception, in her birth, in her life, in her mysteries, in her resurrection and assumption. Her own parents did not know her; and often the angels would ask one another: *Quae est Ista?* "Who is she?" because the Most High had hidden her from them; or, if He did reveal to them anything about her, He concealed infinitely more.

4. God the Father permitted that she should work no miracles during her life, at least no public ones, although He had given her the power to do so. God the Son permitted that she should hardly ever speak, although He had communicated to her His wisdom. God the Holy Ghost, although she was His faithful spouse, permitted that His Apostles and Evangelists should say but very little about her, and then only inasmuch as was necessary to make known Jesus Christ.

5. Mary is the all-excelling masterpiece of the Most High, the knowledge[2] and the possession of which He has reserved

1 Antiphon for Advent. Also *Ave, Maris Stella.*
2 Ut soli Deo cognoscenda reservetur. St Bernardine of Sienna: sermo 51, Art. 1, Cap. 1.

for Himself. Mary is the admirable Mother of the Son, who was pleased to humble and conceal her during her life in order to foster her humility, calling her by the name of "*woman*" (*mulier*),[3] as though she were a stranger; yet in His heart He esteemed and loved her above all angels and men. Mary is the faithful Spouse of the Holy Ghost, and the sealed fountain,[4] to which He alone has access. Mary is the sanctuary and the resting-place of the Blessed Trinity where God dwells more gloriously and more divinely than in any other place in the universe, not excepting His dwelling-place above the Cherubim and Seraphim; nor, without great privilege, is it granted to any creature, no matter how pure, to enter there.

6. I declare with the Saints: the divine Mary[5] is the earthly paradise of the new Adam, wherein He became man by the power of the Holy Ghost, there to work incomprehensible wonders. She is the vast and divine world of God, wherein exist untold beauties and treasures. She is the magnificence of the Most High, wherein He has hidden, as in His own bosom, His only Son, and in Him, all that is most excellent and most precious. Oh! Oh! what great and hidden things Almighty God has wrought in this admirable creature, as she herself was constrained to declare despite her profound humility: *Fecit mihi magna qui potens est.*[6] The world knows them not, because it is incapable and unworthy of such knowledge.

3　John ii, 4; xix, 26.

4　Cant, iv, 12.

5　*Divine Mary.* "This is not the usual way of speaking of Mary, but the word *divine* may be used without attributing the nature of divinity to the person or thing thus qualified. We speak of our prayers, whether addressed to God or to the Saints, as a divine service. Mary may be called divine because divinely chosen for the divine office of the Mother of the divinity. She who was so closely associated with the divinity and overshadowed by it, may be spoken of as divine." (Cardinal Vaughan).

St Thomas says: "Mary, by the fact that she is the Mother of God, has an infinite dignity" (1 Qu. 25, Art. 6).

Cajetan in his Commentary of St Thomas, says: "Mary touches the confines of the divinity, inasmuch as by her proper operation she begot God, and nourished Him at her breast."

6　Luke i, 49. "He that is mighty has done great things to me."

7. The Saints have said wonderful things about this Holy City of God; and, as they themselves declare, never were they more eloquent and more happy than when they spoke of her. Yet they exclaim that the height of her merits, which she has raised to the throne of the Divinity, cannot be perceived; that the breadth of her charity, wider than the earth, cannot be measured; that the greatness of her power, which she possesses over even God Himself, is beyond understanding; and finally, that the depth of her humility, and of all her virtues and graces is an abyss which cannot be sounded. O height incomprehensible! O breadth unspeakable! O greatness immeasurable! O abyss impenetrable!

8. Day by day, from end to end of the earth, in the highest heavens, in the lowest abyss all things preach, all things proclaim the wondrous Mary. The nine choirs of angels, human creatures of whatever sex, age, condition, religion, be they good or evil, and even the demons are compelled by the force of truth, willing or unwilling, to call her Blessed. In heaven, all angels acclaim her unceasingly, as St Bonaventure says: *Sancta, sancta, sancta Maria, Dei Genitrix et Virgo*—"Holy, holy, holy Mary, Mother of God and Virgin";[7] and they greet her millions and millions of times daily with the Angelic Salutation *Ave Maria!* prostrating themselves before her, and begging her as a favour to honour them with some of her commands. According to St Augustine,[8] St Michael himself, though Prince of the heavenly court, is the most zealous in honouring her, and is ever on the alert for the privilege of going, at her word, to the aid of one of her servants.

9. The whole world is filled with her glory, and, in particular, Christian nations have chosen her as guardian and protectress of kingdoms, provinces, dioceses and towns. Numerous

---

7   *Psalter. Majus B.V.*
8   *Speculum B.V.*, lect. iii, 5.

are the cathedrals consecrated to God under her name. There is no church without an altar in her honour, no land or district without one of her miraculous images, where every manner of affliction is healed and every manner of favour obtained. Many are the Confraternities and Congregations in her honour! Many are the religious orders under her name and protection! Countless are the members of her Sodalities and the religious men and women who proclaim her praises and extoll her mercies! There is not a little child who does not praise her with a lisping Hail Mary. There is scarcely a sinner, however obdurate in his sin, who has not retained some spark of confidence in her. There is not even a devil in hell who, whilst fearing her, does not respect her.

10. After all this, in truth we must say with the Saints: *De Maria numquam satis....* We have not yet praised, exalted, honoured, loved and served Mary as we ought to do. She has deserved still more praise, respect, love and service.

11. Moreover we must say with the Holy Ghost: *Omnis gloria ejus filiae Regis ab intus ...*[9] "All the glory of the King's daughter is within": as though all the exterior glory that heaven and earth vie with each other to render her, were as nothing compared with that which she receives interiorly from the Creator; a glory unknown to tiny creatures who cannot penetrate the secret of secrets of the King.

12. Finally we must exclaim with the Apostle: *Nec oculus vidit, nec auris audivit, nec in cor hominis ascendit ...*[10] "Eye hath not seen, nor ear heard, neither hath it entered into the heart of man" what are the beauties, grandeurs and excellences of Mary, the miracle of miracles[11] in the order of grace, of nature and of glory. If you wish to understand the Mother, says a

---

9   Ps. xliv, 14.

10 1 Cor. ii, 9.

11 St John Damascene: *Oratio la de Nativitate.*

Saint,[12] understand the Son. She is a worthy Mother of God: *Hie taceat omnis lingua....* "Here let every tongue be silent."

13. My heart has dictated to me all that I have so joyously written to show that the divine Mary has till now been unknown[13] and that this is one of the reasons why Jesus Christ is not known as He should be. If then, as is certain, the knowledge and kingdom of Jesus Christ come into the world, it will only be as a necessary consequence of the knowledge and reign of the Blessed Virgin Mary. She who first brought Him into the world, will make Him known to the world.

---

12 St Eucharius.

13 *Unknown:* that is, not sufficiently known, as the next words show: "Jesus Christ is not known as He should be."

CHAPTER ONE.

THE NECESSITY OF DEVOTION TO THE BLESSED VIRGIN.

14. With the whole Church I admit that Mary, being but a mere creature from the hands of the Most High, is, in comparison with His infinite Majesty, less than an atom; or rather is just nothing, for He alone is "He who is."[1] Consequently this great Lord, for ever independent and self-sufficient, never had, and has not now any absolute need of the most Blessed Virgin for carrying out His will and for manifesting His glory. He has but to will in order to do all things.

15. I say however that, considering things as they are, considering that God willed to begin and complete His greatest works by the most Blessed Virgin ever since He made her, we can believe that He will never change His plan in future ages, for He is God, and changes neither in His sentiments nor in His way of acting.

ARTICLE I.

Principles.
1st Principle.—God willed to make use of Mary in the Incarnation.

16. God the Father gave His only-begotten Son to the world only through Mary. Whatever sighs the Patriarchs may have uttered, whatever prayers the Prophets and the Saints of the Old Law may have offered for four thousand years to obtain that treasure, it was Mary alone who merited it and found grace before God[2] by the power of her prayers and the

---

1 Exod. iii, 14.
2 Luke i, 30.

eminence of her virtues. The world was unworthy, says St Augustine, to receive the Son of God directly from the hands of the Father, so He gave Him to Mary that the world might receive Him through her.

The Son of God became man for our salvation: but in Mary and by Mary.

God the Holy Ghost formed Jesus Christ in Mary: but after having asked her consent by one of the foremost ministers of His court.

17. God the Father communicated to Mary His fruitfulness, as far as a mere creature was capable of receiving it, to enable her to produce His Son and all the members of His mystical Body.

18. God the Son came down into her virginal womb, as the new Adam into His earthly paradise, to take His delight therein and there to work, in secret, wonders of grace. God made man found His liberty in being imprisoned in her womb; He displayed His power by allowing Himself to be borne by this little maiden; He found His own glory and that of His Father in hiding His splendours from all creatures here below, revealing them to Mary alone. He glorified His independence and His majesty by depending upon this lovable Virgin in His conception, His birth, His presentation in the Temple, in His hidden life of thirty years and even in His death, at which she had to be present, that He might make with her but one same sacrifice, and be immolated, with her consent, to the Eternal Father, just as Isaac was formerly sacrificed with Abraham's consent to the will of God. It is she who suckled him, fed Him, supported Him, reared Him, and sacrificed Him for us.

O admirable and incomprehensible dependence of a God, which the Holy Ghost could not leave unmentioned in the Gospel—although He has hidden from us almost all the wondrous things which the Incarnate Wisdom did during His hidden life—in order to show us its worth and infinite glory. Jesus Christ gave more glory to God, His Father, by His thirty years' submission to His Mother than He would have done in converting the whole world by working the greatest miracles. Oh! how greatly we glorify God when, to please Him, we submit ourselves to Mary after the example of Jesus Christ, our sole model!

19. A close examination of the remainder of the life of Jesus Christ shows us that He willed to begin His miracles through Mary. By her word, He sanctified St John in the womb of his mother St Elizabeth; no sooner had she spoken than John was sanctified: this was His first and greatest miracle in the order of grace. At her humble prayer, He changed water into wine at the marriage feast of Cana; this was His first miracle in the order of nature. He began and He continued His miracles by Mary, and to the end of time He will continue them by her.

20. God the Holy Ghost being barren in God, that is, producing no other Divine Person, became fruitful by Mary, whom He espoused. It is with her and in her and of her that He produced His masterpiece, God made man, and with her and in her daily to the end of time He produces the predestinate and the members of the Body of this adorable Head. It is for this reason that the more He finds Mary, His dear and inseparable Spouse in a soul,[3] the more active and powerful He becomes to produce Jesus Christ in that soul, and that soul in Jesus Christ.

21. This does not mean that the Blessed Virgin gives fruitfulness to the Holy Ghost, as if He did not possess it; for, being God, He has like the Father and the Son, fruitfulness

---

3 St Ildefonse: *Liber de Corona Virginis.* Cap. iii. St Robert Bellarmine: *Concio 2ª super Missus est.*

or the capacity to produce, although He does not put it into act, since He produces no other Divine Person. But it means that through the Blessed Virgin whom He deigns to use, without absolutely needing her, the Holy Ghost puts into act His fruitfulness, producing in her and by her Jesus Christ and His members: a mystery of grace unknown even to the most learned and spiritual of Christians.

2nd Principle.—God wishes to make use of Mary in the Sanctification of souls.

22. The plan that the three Persons of the Blessed Trinity followed in the Incarnation, the first coming of Jesus Christ, They still follow each day in an invisible manner throughout Holy Church, and They will pursue it to the end of time, in the last coming of Jesus Christ.

23. God the Father made an assemblage of all waters and He called it the sea; He made an assemblage of all His graces and He called it Mary.[4] This great God has a treasure house, a most wealthy store, in which He has enclosed all that is beautiful, resplendent, rare and precious, even His own Son; and this immense treasury is none other than Mary, whom the Saints call the treasure house of the Lord,[5] from the plenitude of which all men are made rich.

24. God the Son communicated to His Mother all that He acquired by His life and death, His infinite merits and His admirable virtues; and He made her the Treasurer of all that His Father gave Him as heritage. By her He applies His merits to His members; by her He communicates His virtues and distributes His graces. She is His mysterious channel, His aqueduct, through which He makes His mercies flow gently and abundantly.

---

4 Appelavit eam Mariam, quasi mare gratiarum. St Antoninus: *Summa.* P. iv, Tit. 15, Cap. iv.
5 Ipsa est thesaurus Domini. Idiota: *In contemplatione B.M.V.*

25. God the Holy Ghost communicated His unspeakable gifts to Mary, His faithful Spouse, and He chose her as the dispensatrix of all He possesses; so that she distributes all His gifts and graces to whom she wills, in the measure she wills, how she wills and when she wills; nor does He give any heavenly gift to man which does not pass through her virginal hands. For such is the will of God who has decreed that we should have all things through Mary, so that she who made herself poor and lowly and hid herself in an abyss of nothingness by her profound humility during her whole life, might thus be enriched, exalted and honoured by the Most High. Such are the views of the Church and the Holy Fathers.[6]

26. Were I speaking to the free-thinkers of these times, I would prove at greater length all that I now state so simply, by the Sacred Scriptures, by the Holy Fathers of whom I would give the Latin quotations; and also by solid arguments which can be seen in full in Fr. Poiré's book: *La Triple Couronne de la Sainte Vierge* (The threefold Crown of the Blessed Virgin). But as I speak particularly for the poor and simple, who, being of good will, and having more faith than the generality of learned men, believe more simply and more meritoriously, I am content to state the truth to them with simplicity, without stopping to quote the Latin passages which they would not understand. Nevertheless, I shall quote some of these texts without, however, going out of my way to do so. But to continue.

27. Inasmuch as grace perfects nature and glory perfects grace, it is certain that Our Lord remains in heaven just as much the Son of Mary as He was on earth; and that, consequently, He has retained the submission and obedience of the most perfect of all children towards the best of all mothers. But we must take care not to consider this dependence

---

6 Cf. St Bernard and St Bernardine, quoted by De Montfort in Nos. 141 and 142.

as an abasement or imperfection in Jesus Christ. For Mary, infinitely inferior to her Son who is God, does not command Him as an earthly mother commands her child who is inferior to her. Mary, completely transformed in God by that grace and glory which transforms all the Saints in Him, neither asks, wishes nor does anything contrary to the eternal and unchangeable Will of God. When, therefore, we read in the writings of St Bernard, St Bernardine, St Bonaventure, etc., that in heaven and on earth all, even God Himself, is subject to the Blessed Virgin,[7] they mean this: the authority which God has been pleased to give her is so great that she seems to have the same power as God; her prayers and requests are so powerful with Him that they are taken as commands by the Divine Majesty, who never resists His dear Mother's prayer because it is always humble and conformed to His Will.

If Moses, by the power of his prayer, curbed God's anger against the Israelites so effectively that the Most High and infinitely merciful Lord, unable to withstand him, asked him to let Him grow angry and punish that rebellious people, what then must we not think, with all the more reason, of the prayer of the humble Mary, worthy Mother of God, which is more powerful with His Majesty than the prayers and intercession of all the Angels and Saints in heaven and on earth?[8]

28. In heaven Mary commands the Angels and the Blessed. In reward for her profound humility, God has given her the power and office of filling with Saints the empty thrones from which the apostate angels fell by pride.[9] Such is the will of the Most High who exalts the humble,[10] that heaven, earth and hell, willingly or unwillingly, should comply with the com-

---

7 Cf. quotation in No. 76.
8 St Augustine: Sermo 208 *In Assumptione* (inter opera S Augustini).
9 Per Mariam ab hominibus angelorum chori reintegrantur. *Speculum B.V. lect. XI,* 6.
10 Luke i, 52.

mands of the humble Mary,[11] whom He has made Sovereign of heaven and earth, General of His armies, Keeper of His treasures, Dispensatrix of His graces, Worker of His wonders, Restorer of the human race, Mediatrix of men, Destroyer of the enemies of God and loyal companion of His greatness and His triumphs.

29. God the Father wishes to make for Himself children by Mary till the end of time, and to her He says these words: *In Jacob inhabita* ... "Dwell in Jacob"[12] that is to say, take up thy dwelling and abode in my children, in my predestinate, prefigured by Jacob, and not in the children of the devil, in the reprobate, prefigured by Esau.

30. Just as in natural and corporal generation, there is a father and a mother, so in the supernatural and spiritual generation there is a Father, who is God, and a Mother, who is Mary. All true children of God, the predestinate, have God for their Father and Mary for their Mother; and he who has not Mary for his Mother, has not God for his Father. This is why the reprobate, such as heretics, schismatics, etc., who hate, despise or ignore the Blessed Virgin, do not have God for their Father, though they glory that they have, because Mary is not their Mother. Indeed, if they had her for their Mother, they would love and honour her as a good and true child naturally loves and honours the mother who gave him life.

The most infallible and unmistakable sign by which we may distinguish a heretic, a man of false doctrine, a reprobate, from a predestinate soul, is that the heretic and the reprobate show only contempt or indifference for Our Lady,[13] and strive by word and example, openly or secretly, to diminish love and

11 In nomine tuo omne genu flectatur caelestium, terrestrium et infernorum. St Bonaventure. *(Psalt. Maj. B.V, Cant, instar Cantici trium puerorum).*
12 Eccli. xxiv, 13.
13 Quicumque vult salvus esse, ante omnia opus est ut teneat de Maria firmam fidem. St Bonaventure *(Psalt. Majus B.V. Symbolum instar Symboli Athanasii).*

veneration for her, sometimes under specious pretexts. Alas! God the Father has not told Mary to take up her dwelling in them, because they are other Esaus.

31. God the Son wishes to form Himself and, so to speak, to become incarnate every day through His Blessed Mother, in His members; to her He says: *In Israel hereditare....* "Let thy inheritance be in Israel;"[14] as if He said: God My Father has given Me for heritage all the nations of the earth, all men good or bad, predestinate and reprobate; the former I will rule with a rod of gold and the latter with a rod of iron; to the former I shall be a Father and Advocate, to the latter the Just Avenger; of them all I shall be Judge. But you, dear Mother, will have for your heritage and possession only the predestinate, prefigured by Israel; as their Mother you will bear them, nourish them, rear them; as their Sovereign you will lead, govern and defend them.

32. "This man and that man is born of her," says the Holy Ghost ... *Homo et homo natus est in ea.*[15] According to the explanation of some of the Fathers,[16] the first man that is born of Mary is the Man-God, Jesus Christ; the second is mere man, the child of God and of Mary by adoption. If Jesus Christ, the Head of mankind, is born in her, the predestinate, who are members of this Head, must also, by a necessary consequence, be born in her. One and the same mother does not bring forth the head without the members, nor the members without the head; it would be a monster in the order of nature. In the order of grace likewise the Head and the members are born of the same Mother; and if a member of the mystical Body of Christ, that is, one of the predestinate, were born of any other mother than Mary who has brought forth the Head, he would not be one of the predestinate, nor a member of Jesus Christ, but a monster in the order of grace.

14   Eccli. xxiv, 13.
15   Ps. lxxxvi, 5.
16   Origen, St Bonaventure and others. Cf. No. 141.

33. Further, Jesus being still as much as ever the Fruit of Mary, as heaven and earth repeat thousands of time a day: "*and blessed is the Fruit of thy womb, Jesus,*" it is certain that for every man in particular who possesses Him, Jesus is as much the Fruit and the work of Mary as He is for the whole world in general; so that if any of the faithful have Jesus Christ formed in their hearts, they can boldly say: "Thanks be to Mary! What I possess is her Product and her Fruit, and without her I would not have Him." We can say more truly of her than St Paul said of himself: *Quos iterum parturio donec formetur Christus in vobis....*[17] I am in labour again with all the children of God, until Jesus Christ my Son be formed in them to the fulness of His age. St Augustine,[18] surpassing himself and all that I have yet said, affirms that to be conformed to the image of the Son of God, all the predestinate are in this world hidden in the bosom of the Blessed Virgin, where they are protected, nourished, cared for and developed by this good Mother, until after death—called by the Church the birthday of the just—she brings them forth to a life of glory. O mystery of grace; unknown to the reprobate, and but little known to the predestinate!

34. God the Holy Ghost wishes to raise up for Himself elect in her and by her, and He says to her: *In electis meis mitte radices.*[19] My well-beloved, My Spouse, place the roots of all thy virtues in My elect, that they may grow from virtue to virtue and from grace to grace. When thou wert living on earth in the practice of the most sublime Virtues, I was so well pleased in thee that I still desire to find thee on earth, without thy ceasing to be in heaven. Reproduce thyself, then, in My elect so that with delight I may see in them the roots of thine invincible faith, profound humility, universal mortification, sublime prayer, ardent charity, firm hope and all thy virtues.

---

17 Gal. iv, 19.
18 *Tract, de Symbolo ad Catechumenos.*
19 Eccli. xxiv, 13.

Thou art ever My Spouse, as faithful, as pure and as fruitful as ever. Let thy faith give Me faithful, thy purity virgins, thy fruitfulness temples and elect.

35. When Mary has taken root in a soul, she produces in it wonders of grace which she alone can produce for she alone is the fruitful Virgin who has never had and never will have her equal in purity and fruitfulness.

With the Holy Ghost Mary produced the greatest thing that ever was or ever will be: a God-Man; she will produce, consequently, the greatest things that will come to be in the latter times. The formation and education of the great saints who will live at the end of the world is reserved to her, for only this singular and miraculous Virgin can produce, in union with the Holy Ghost, singular and extraordinary things.

36. When the Holy Ghost, her Spouse, finds Mary in a soul, He flies there and enters fully; He communicates Himself to that soul in abundance and to the extent that it makes room for His Spouse. One of the chief reasons why the Holy Ghost does not now work striking wonders in souls is that He fails to find in them a sufficiently close union with His faithful and inseparable Spouse. I say inseparable Spouse, for from the moment the Substantial Love of the Father and the Son espoused Mary to form Jesus Christ, the Head of the elect, and Jesus Christ in the elect, He has never repudiated her, for at all times she has been faithful and fruitful.

ARTICLE II.

Consequences.
1st Consequence.—Mary is the Queen of our hearts.

37. We must evidently conclude from what I have just said:
Firstly, that Mary has received from God a far-reaching dominion over the souls of the elect, otherwise she could not

make in them her dwelling-place as God the Father has ordered her to do; nor as their Mother, form, nourish and bring them forth to eternal life; nor have them for her heritage and possession forming them in Jesus Christ and Jesus Christ in them; nor place the roots of her virtues in their hearts and be the inseparable companion of the Holy Ghost in all His works of grace... none of these things, I repeat, could she do unless she had right and dominion over their souls by a singular grace of the Most High, who, having given her power over His Only-Begotten and Natural Son, has also given her power over His adopted children, not only over their bodies, which would be but little, but also over their souls.

38. Mary is the Queen of heaven and earth by grace, as Jesus is their King by nature and by conquest. Now just as the Kingdom of Jesus Christ is chiefly in the heart or interior of man, according to these words: "The Kingdom of God is within you,"[20] even so, the Kingdom of Our Blessed Lady is chiefly in the interior of man, that is, in his soul; and it is chiefly in souls that she is more glorified with her Son than in all visible creatures; and with the Saints we can call her *the Queen of our hearts.*

2nd Consequence.—Mary is necessary to men to attain their final end.

39. Secondly, we must conclude that as the Blessed Virgin is necessary to God—that is to say, hypothetically necessary, because He so willed it—she is far more necessary to men in the attainment of their last end. Consequently, devotion to her is not to be confused with devotion to the other Saints, as if it were not more necessary and simply a matter of supererogation.

---

20 Luke xvii, 21.

I. Devotion to Our Blessed Lady is necessary to all for salvation.

40. The pious and learned Suarez, of the Com pany of Jesus, the devout and erudite Justus Lipsius, Doctor of Louvain, and many others have established beyond opposition that devotion to Our Blessed Lady is necessary for salvation. This they prove from the teaching of the Fathers, notably St Augustine, St Ephrem, Deacon of Edessa, St Cyril of Jerusalem, St Germanus of Constantinople, St John Damascene, St Anselm, St Bernard, St Bernardine, St Thomas and St Bonaventure. Further, they show that even in the opinion of Oecolampadius and other heretics, a lack of esteem and love for Mary is an infallible sign of reprobation; whilst to be truly and completely devoted to her is an infallible sign of predestination.

41. The types and texts of the Old and New Testament prove this. The opinions and examples of the Saints confirm it. Reason and experience teach and demonstrate it; even the devil and his wicked angels, driven by the strength of truth, have been frequently obliged, against their will, to admit it. For brevity's sake I shall quote but one of the many passages which I have collected from the Fathers and the Doctors of the Church in support of this truth: *Tibi devotum esse, est arma quaedam salutis quae Deus his dat, quos vult salvos fieri....* "To have devotion to thee, O Blessed Virgin, is an arm of salvation which God gives to those whom He wishes to save," says St John Damascene.

42. I could here bring forward many stories which prove this same truth, among them: (1) That which is related in the Chronicles of St Francis of how he saw in an ecstasy an immense ladder reaching to heaven, at the top of which was Our Blessed Lady; and by Which, he was told, we must go up to heaven. (2) That which is related in the Chronicles of St Dominic. Near Carcassonne, where St Dominic was preaching the Rosary, there was an unfortunate heretic possessed by fifteen thousand devils. These evil spirits were compelled at the command of Our Lady to confess, to their confusion, many great and consoling truths concerning devotion to her; and with such force and clarity that, if we have any devotion to her, we cannot, without shedding tears of joy, read this authentic story and the unwilling homage that the devil paid to devotion to Our Lady.

II. Devotion to Our Lady is even more necessary to those who are called to a special perfection.

43. If devotion to the most Blessed Virgin Mary is necessary to all men, merely to work out their salvation, it is even more so to those who are called to a special perfection. I do not think that anyone can acquire intimate union with Our Lord and perfect fidelity to the Holy Ghost, without a very close union with the most Blessed Virgin and a great dependence on her aid.

44. Mary alone found grace with God,[21] without the help of any other creature. Since then, all who have found grace with God have done so through her, all who are still to come will find it through her. She was full of grace when she was greeted by the Archangel Gabriel,[22] and she was superabundantly filled with grace by the Holy Ghost when He overshadowed her;[23] and this twofold plenitude she so increased from day to day, from moment to moment that she has reached an immense, an inconceivable degree of grace. So much so that the Most High has made her the sole custodian of His treasures, the unique dispensatrix of His graces that she may ennoble, raise, and enrich whomsoever she wishes; put on the narrow path to heaven whomsoever she wishes; bring through

---

21 Luke i, 30.
22 Luke i, 28.
23 Luke i, 35.

that narrow gate of Life, in spite of all obstacles, and give the royal throne, crown and sceptre to whomsoever she wishes. Jesus is everywhere and always the Fruit and the Son of Mary; and Mary is everywhere the genuine tree which bears the Fruit of Life, and the true Mother who produces it....[24]

45. To Mary alone God gave the keys of the cellars[25] of divine love, the power to enter the most sublime and secret ways of perfection, and the power to bring others into these ways. Mary alone gives to the miserable children of faithless Eve entry into the earthly paradise, there to walk pleasantly with God, to be safely hidden from their enemies; to feed with delight on the fruit of the trees of life and knowledge of good and evil, without fear of death; there to drink copiously of the heavenly waters of that beauteous fountain which gushes there with such abundance. Or rather, as she is herself the earthly paradise, that virgin and blessed earth from which sinful Adam and Eve were driven forth, she admits only those she pleases, in order to make them saints.

46. "All the rich among the people," to make use of the words of the Holy Ghost,[26] according to the explanation of St Bernard—all the rich among the people will entreat thy countenance from age to age, particularly as the world draws to its close. That is to say, the greatest saints, those souls richest in grace and virtue, will be the most persistent in praying to Our Blessed Lady, in having her ever present as their perfect model to be imitated and as their powerful aid to assist them.

47. I have said that this would come to pass particularly as the world draws to its close—and indeed soon[27]—for the Most

---

24   Cf. No. 33.
25   Cant, i, 3.
26   Ps. xliv, 13.
27   Montfort, like other pious men of his time, may have thought that the end of the world was not far off. More probably, however, he meant that this would come to pass especially at the end of the world, and would begin soon; and indeed the century which followed his own was noted for a great increase in devotion to Our Lady.

High and His Blessed Mother are to raise up for themselves great saints who will as much surpass in sanctity most other saints as the cedars of Lebanon tower above little shrubs—as has been revealed to a saintly soul whose life has been written by M. de Renty.[28]

48. These great souls, filled with grace and zeal, will be chosen to stand against the enemies of God, raging on all sides. They will be outstandingly devoted to the Blessed Virgin, illuminated by her light, nourished with her milk, led by her spirit, supported by her arm and sheltered beneath her protection, so that whilst with the one hand they will fight, with the other they will build.[29] With the one hand they will fight, overcome and crush heretics and their heresies, schismatics and their schisms, idolaters and their idolatries, sinners and their wickedness. With the other hand they will build the temple of the true Solomon and the Mystical City of God, which are none other than the most Blessed Virgin, called by the Holy Fathers the *Temple of Solomon*[30] and the *City of God*.[31] By word and example they will make all men truly devoted to her, and, though this will make numerous enemies, it will also bring them many victories, and procure much glory for God alone. This was revealed by God to St Vincent Ferrer, the outstanding apostle of his century, as he has sufficiently pointed out in one of his works.

This seems also to have been foretold by the Holy Ghost in the 58th Psalm. Here are the words: Et scient quia Dominus dominabitur Jacob, et finium terrae; convertentur ad vesperas, et famem patientur ut canes, et circuibunt civitatem ... "And they shall know that God will rule Jacob and all the ends of

---

28 This saintly soul was Marie des Vallées of whom St John Eudes was the Spiritual Director.

29 2 Esdras iv, 17.

30 Ps. lviii, 14-15.

31 Ps. lxxxvi, 3.

the earth; they shall return at evening and shall suffer hunger like dogs and shall go round about the city looking for food." This city, round which men will roam at the end of the world, seeking conversion and appeasement of the hunger they feel for justice, is the most Blessed Virgin, called by the Holy Ghost the City of God.

III. Devotion to Our Blessed Lady will be more particularly necessary in the latter times.

A. Special role of Mary in the latter times.

49. By Mary was the salvation of the world begun, and by Mary it must be consummated. Mary scarcely appeared in the first coming of Christ, so that men, insufficiently instructed and enlightened concerning the Person of her Son, might not leave the path of truth by attaching themselves too strongly and too grossly to her. This would apparently have happened if she had been known, because of the wondrous charms which the Most High had bestowed even on her outward appearance. So true is this that St Denys the Areopagite tells us in his writings that when he saw her, he would have taken her for a divinity because of her secret charms and incomparable beauty, had not his firm faith taught him the contrary.[32] But in the second coming of Jesus Christ, Mary must be made known and revealed by the Holy Ghost so that through her Jesus Christ may be known, loved and served. The reasons which moved the Holy Ghost to hide His Spouse during her life and to reveal her but very little since the preaching of the Gospel, exist no longer.

50. God, then, wishes to reveal and make known Mary, the masterpiece of His hands, in these latter times.

1. Because she hid herself in this world and in her deep humility rated herself lower than the dust, having obtained

---

32 *Epistola ad St Paulum.*

from God, His apostles and His evangelists, the favour of not being made known.

2. Because as Mary is the masterpiece of God's hands, as much here below by grace as in heaven by glory, He wishes to be glorified and praised because of her by those who are on earth.

3. As she is the dawn which precedes and discloses Jesus Christ, the Sun of Justice, she must be known and seen, that Jesus Christ may be known and seen.

4. As she was the way by which Jesus Christ first came to us, she will be the way by which He will come the second time, though not in the same manner.

5. As she is the sure means, the straight and immaculate way to go to Jesus and to find Him perfectly, it is through her that souls who are to blossom forth in sanctity must find Him. Whosoever will find Mary will find Life,[33] that is, Jesus Christ, Who is the Way, the Truth and the Life.[34] But Mary cannot be found without search; you cannot seek for what you do not know, for you neither seek nor desire a thing unknown. It is imperative therefore that Mary should be more known than ever, for the better understanding and the greater glory of the Most Blessed Trinity.

6. In these latter times Mary must more than ever shine forth in mercy, in power, and in grace. In mercy, that she may lead back and lovingly receive poor sinners and wanderers who are to be converted and return to the Catholic Church. In power, against the enemies of God: idolaters, schismatics, Mahometans, Jews and hardened impious men who will rise in terrible revolt seeking to seduce and bring down, by promises and threats, all who oppose them. And finally, she must shine forth in grace, to animate and support

---

33 Prov. viii, 35.
34 John xiv, 6.

the valiant soldiers and faithful servants of Jesus Christ who fight for His interest.

7. Finally; Mary must be as terrible as an army in battle array to the devil and his followers, particularly in the latter times;[35] for the devil knowing full well that he has little time—less than ever[36]—to damn souls, redoubles every day his efforts and his attacks; he will soon give rise to cruel persecutions and lay terrible snares for the faithful servants and true children of Mary, whom he finds more difficult to overcome than the rest.

51. It is chiefly in reference to these last cruel persecutions of the devil, daily increasing until the reign of Antichrist, that we should understand the first and outstanding prophecy and curse of God, uttered against the serpent in the earthly paradise. It is opportune to explain it here, for the glory of the most Blessed Virgin, for the salvation of her children and the confusion of the devil.

Inimicitias ponam inter te et mulierem, et semen tuum et semen illius; ipsa conteret caput tuum et tu insidiaberis calcaneo ejus … "I will put enmities between thee and the woman, and thy seed and her seed; she shall crush thy head, and thou shalt lie in wait for her heel." (Gen. iii, 15.)

52. God has made and set up only one enmity but it is irreconcilable, lasting and increasing even to the end. And that enmity is between Mary, His worthy Mother and the devil, between her children and servants and the children and followers of Lucifer. Thus, the most terrible enemy that God has raised up against Satan, is Mary, His Holy Mother. From the time of the earthly Paradise, though she existed then only in His mind, He gave her such hatred of this accursed enemy

---

35 It may be noted that in our days when the devil is renewing all his efforts and organising the legions of his ministers in the world, we also witness an unprecedented increase in devotion to Our Lady.

36 Apoc. xii, 12.

of God, such skill in exposing the malice of the ancient serpent, such strength to overcome, cast down and crush this proud rebel that he fears her not only more than all angels and men, but in a certain sense, more than God Himself. This does not mean that the anger, hatred and power of God are not infinitely greater than those of Mary, for her perfections are limited; but Satan fears her more than God because, firstly, in his pride, he suffers infinitely more from being conquered and punished by a small and humble handmaid of God; her humility humiliates him more than the power of God. Secondly, because God has given Mary such power over the evil spirits that, as they themselves have often unwillingly admitted through the mouths of the possessed, they fear but one of her sighs for a soul more than the prayers of all the saints, and but one of her threats more than all their other torments.

53. What Lucifer lost by pride, Mary won by humility. What Eve damned and lost by disobedience, Mary saved by obedience. Eve by obeying the serpent lost with herself her children and delivered them into his power. Mary by her perfect fidelity to God saved with herself all her children and servants and consecrated them to His Divine Majesty.

54. God has put not only enmity, *but enmities;* not only between Mary and Satan, but between her race and his race; that is, God has put enmities, antipathies and secret hatreds between the true children and servants of Our Blessed Lady and the children and slaves of the Devil. They have no love for each other; there is no interior agreement between them. The children of Belial, the slaves of Satan, the lovers of this world—for it is all one and the same thing—have always persecuted and will persecute more than ever those who belong to the Blessed Virgin; just as Cain of old persecuted his brother Abel, and Esau his brother Jacob, who are types of the reprobate and the predestinate. But the humble Mary will always be victorious over this proud serpent, so strikingly that she will even crush his head—the seat of his pride. She will always unmask his serpent's cunning, she will expose his infernal traps, she will scatter to the winds his devilish counsels and to the end of time will safeguard her faithful servants from his cruel claw. But Mary's mastery of Hell will shine forth especially in the latter times, when Satan will lie in wait for her heel, that is, for her humble slaves and her poor children whom she will rouse to war against him. In the eyes of the world they will be little and poor, and like the heel they will be lowly in the eyes of all, down-trodden and persecuted as is the heel by the other members of the body. But to compensate this they will be rich in the grace of God, abundantly bestowed on them by Mary; by their sanctity they will be great and exalted before God; by their lively zeal they will be superior to all creatures, and so strongly will they be upheld by Divine assistance, that with the lowliness of their heel, in union with Mary, they will crush the head of Satan and bring victory to Jesus Christ.

B. *The Apostles of the latter times.*

55. Finally, God wishes His Blessed Mother to be now more known, more loved and more honoured than she has ever been. This will doubtless come to pass if, with the grace and light of the Holy Ghost, the predestinate enter into the interior and perfect practice which I shall later unfold. Then will they see clearly, as much as faith allows, that beautiful Star of the Sea and under her guidance will come safely to harbour, in spite of storms and pirates. They will perceive the grandeurs of this Queen and will consecrate themselves entirely to her service, as subjects and slaves of love. They will taste of her sweetness and maternal goodness, and like beloved children will love her tenderly. They will acknowledge her plenitude of mercy and the need in which they stand of her help: in all things they will

have recourse to her as to their dear advocate and mediatrix
with Jesus Christ. They will realise that she is the easiest, the
shortest, the most perfect means of approaching Jesus Christ
and will surrender themselves to her, soul and body, without
reserve, in order to belong entirely to Jesus Christ.

56. But who will be these servants, these slaves, these children of Mary?

They will be a burning fire:[37] ministers of the Lord, who
will enkindle everywhere the fires of Divine Love.

They will be *sicut sagittae in manu potentis,*[38] sharp arrows
in the strong hands of Mary wherewith to transfix her enemies.

They will be the children of Levi, purified by the fire of
great tribulation and closely joined to the Lord,[39] carrying
the gold of love in their hearts, the incense of prayer in their
mind, the myrrh of mortification in their body; bringing everywhere the good odour of Jesus Christ to the poor and the
little, but the odour of death to the great, the rich and proud
worldlings.

57. They will be thundering clouds, flying through the air
at the least breath of the Holy Ghost. Attached to nothing,
astonished at nothing, troubled at nothing, they will show-
er forth the rain of God's word and of life eternal. They will
thunder against sin, they will storm against the world, they
will strike down the devil and his followers, and, for life or
for death, they will pierce through and through with the two-
edged sword of God's Word,[40] all those to whom they are sent
on behalf of the Most High.

58. They will be true apostles of the latter times to whom
the Lord of Hosts will give speech and strength to work won-

---

37 Ps. ciii, 4 and Luke xii, 49.
38 Ps. cxxvi, 4.
39 Deut. x, 15.
40 Eph. vi, 17.

ders and carry off glorious spoil from His enemies. They will sleep without gold or silver, and what is more important, without worry, in the midst of other priests, ecclesiastics and clerics, *inter medics cleros*,[41] and yet they will have the silver wings of the dove to go wherever the Holy Ghost calls them, filled with the pure intention of the glory of God and the salvation of souls. Where they have preached they will leave only the gold of charity which is the fulfilment of the whole law.[42]

59. Lastly, we know they will be true disciples of Jesus Christ, walking in the steps of His poverty, His humility, His contempt of the world and His charity, teaching the strait way of God, in pure truth, according to the Holy Gospel and not according to the maxims of the world; without worrying about anyone, without favouring anyone, without sparing, heeding or fearing any mortal, however powerful he may be. In their mouths they will have the double-edged sword of the Word of God, on their shoulders will be the bloodstained standard of the Cross, in their right hand the crucifix, in their left the rosary, on their hearts the sacred names of Jesus and Mary, and in their whole behaviour the modesty and mortification of Jesus Christ.[43]

Such are the great men who are to come, fashioned by Mary at the command of the Most High in order to extend His empire over that of the ungodly, the idolaters, and the Mahometans. But when and how will this be done? ... God alone knows;[44] for our part we must be silent, we must pray, sigh and wait: *Exspectans exspectavi.*[45]

---

41 Ps. lxvii, 14.
42 Rom. xiii, 10.
43 This description of the apostles of the latter times reminds us of what De Montfort says in his ardent prayer, asking for Missionaries for his Company of Mary.
44 This last remark shows that De Montfort himself was much in the dark about the details of his own prophecy.
45 Ps. xxxix, 2.

CHAPTER TWO.

FUNDAMENTAL TRUTHS CONCERNING DEVOTION TO OUR BLESSED LADY.

60. Having thus far spoken briefly of the necessity of devotion to Our Blessed Lady, I must now state in what this devotion consists. This I will do, with God's help, when I have laid down certain fundamental truths, which will throw light on this great and solid devotion which I desire to disclose.

ARTICLE I.

Jesus Christ is the ultimate end of devotion to Our Lady.

61. *First Truth.*—Jesus Christ, our Saviour, true God and true man, must be the ultimate end of all our other devotions; otherwise they would be false and misleading. Jesus Christ is the *alpha* and *omega*,[1] the beginning and end of all things. We labour not, as the Apostle says, except to make all men perfect in Jesus Christ, because in Him alone dwells the entire plenitude of the Divinity, and all other plenitudes of graces, of virtues and of perfections; because in Him alone we have been blessed with every spiritual blessing; because He alone is the Master who must teach us; our only Lord, on whom we must depend; our only Head, to whom we must be united; our only Model, to which we must conform ourselves; our only Physician, who must heal us; our only Shepherd, who must feed us; our only Way, who must lead us, our only Truth, in whom we must believe; our only Life, who must animate us; and our only All in all things, who must satisfy us. There is no other name under heaven, but the name of Jesus by which we must

---

1 The substance of the next few pages is taken from Scripture, principally from St John and St Paul.

be saved. God has laid no other foundation of our salvation, of our perfection, and of our glory, than Jesus Christ. Every edifice which is not built on that firm rock is founded upon shifting sand, and sooner or later will infallibly fall. Every one of the faithful who is not united to Him as is a branch to the stem of the vine, shall fall, wither and be fit only to be cast into the fire. Without Him, all is but straying, lying, iniquity, futility, death and damnation. If we are in Jesus Christ and Jesus Christ is in us, we need not fear damnation. Neither angels from heaven nor the men of this earth, nor devils from hell, nor any other creature can harm us, for they cannot separate us from the love of God, which is in Jesus Christ. By Jesus Christ, with Jesus Christ, in Jesus Christ, we can do all things: render all honour and glory to the Father in the unity of the Holy Ghost;[2] become perfect ourselves, and be to our neighbour the good odour of eternal life.[3]

62. If, then, we are establishing solid devotion to Our Blessed Lady, it is only to establish more "perfectly devotion to Jesus Christ, to provide an easy and sure means of finding Jesus Christ. Did devotion to Our Lady draw us away from Jesus Christ, we would have to reject it as an illusion of the devil; but so far is this from being the case, that on the contrary, as I have already shown and as I shall show, this devotion is necessary for us only to find Jesus Christ perfectly, to love Him tenderly and to serve Him faithfully.

63. Here I turn for a moment to Thee, O my Sweet Jesus, in loving plaint before Thy Divine Majesty, that most Christians, even the most learned, do not know the necessary union that exists between Thee and Thy Blessed Mother. Lord, Thou art always with Mary and Mary is always with Thee, nor can she be without Thee, else she would cease to be what she is.

---

2   Canon Missae.
3   2 Cor. ii, 15-16.

So much is she transformed by grace into Thee that she no longer lives, she no longer is; Thou alone, My Jesus, livest and reignest in her, more perfectly than in all the angels and the blessed. Ah! did we but know the glory and the love which Thou receivest in this admirable creature, we would have for Thee and for her feelings far different from those we now possess. So intimately is she united to Thee, that it would be easier to separate light from the sun, heat from fire, nay, it would be easier to separate from Thee all the angels and saints than the divine Mary, for she loves Thee more ardently and glorifies Thee more perfectly than all Thy creatures put together.

64. In view of this, my sweet Master, is it not astonishing and pitiable to see the ignorance and darkness of all men here below with regard to Thy Holy Mother? I speak not so much of idolaters, and pagans, who, not knowing Thee, are far from knowing her. I do not even speak of heretics and schismatics, who are far from being devoted to Thy Holy Mother, separated as they are from Thee and from Thy Holy Church; but I speak of Catholics, and even of doctors among them,[4] who, professing to teach truth to others, know neither Thee nor Thy Holy Mother, except in a speculative, dry, sterile and indifferent manner. These gentlemen speak but rarely of Thy Holy Mother and the devotion we must have to her, because, they say, it will be misused, and Thou wilt be insulted by excessive honour to Thy Mother. If they see or hear a devout servant of Mary speak frequently of devotion to this good Mother in terms that are tender, strong and persuasive, saying that it is a sure means without illusion, a short path free from danger; an immaculate way free from imperfection, and a wondrous secret of finding and loving Thee perfectly, they cry out against him and put before him a thousand false reasons by way of

---

4 De Montfort wrote at a Jansenistic period when even some learned men were opposed to Devotion to Our Lady-Cf. No. 93.

proving that he must not speak so much of the Blessed Virgin, that there are in this devotion great abuses, which he should try to stamp out, and that he should speak of Thee rather than bring people to devotion to the Blessed Virgin, for whom they already have sufficient love.

They are sometimes heard speaking of devotion to Thy Holy Mother, not for the purpose of establishing it and convincing people of it, but to destroy the abuses which are made of it. Yet all the while these gentlemen are devoid of piety and tender devotion to Thee, for they have no devotion to Mary, looking upon the Rosary, the Scapular and the Chaplet as old women's devotions, suited only to the ignorant, and unnecessary for salvation. If they come across any client of Our Lady who says the Rosary, or has some other practice of devotion towards her, they speedily change his mind and his heart. In place of the Rosary, they will advise him to say the seven penitential psalms; in place of devotion to the Blessed Virgin, they will advise devotion to Jesus Christ.

O my sweet Jesus, do these people possess Thy spirit? Do they please Thee by acting in this manner? Does it please Thee that we should not make any effort to give pleasure to Thy Mother for fear of offending Thee? Does devotion to Thy Mother hinder devotion to Thee? Does she attribute to herself the honour we pay her? Does she keep aloof from Thee? Is she a stranger having no contact with Thee? Is the wish to please her displeasing to Thee? Is the gift of oneself to her, love for her, a separation, a wandering from Thy love?

65. Yet, my sweet Master, the greater number of learned men, in punishment for their pride, could not draw further away from devotion to Thy Mother nor show more indifference to it, even if all I have just said were true. Keep me, Lord, keep me from, their opinions and their practices, and let me share in the feelings of gratitude, esteem, respect and love that

Thou hast for Thy Holy Mother, so that I may love and glorify Thee all the more as I shall be imitating and following Thee more closely.

66. As though I had said nothing so far in honour of Thy Holy Mother, grant me now the grace to praise her worthily; *Fac me digne tuam matrem collaudare,* in defiance of all her enemies who are Thine also; and let me say boldly to them with the Saints: *Non praesumat aliquis Deum se habere propitium qui benedictam matrem offensam habuerit …*[5] "Let no one presume to look for the mercy of God who offends His Holy Mother."

67. And to obtain from Thy mercy a true devotion to Thy Blessed Mother and to breathe it into the whole world, make me love Thee ardently and to that end do Thou receive the burning prayer which I offer with St Augustine[6] and all who truly love Thee:

Tu es Christus, pater meus sanctus, Deus meus pius, rex meus magnus, pastor meus bonus, magister meus unus, adjutor meus optimus, dilectus meus pulcherrimus, panis meus vivus, sacerdos meus in aeternum, dux meus ad patriam, lux mea vera, dulcedo mea sancta, via mea recta, sapientia mea praeclara, simplicitas mea pura, concordia mea pacifica, custodia mea tota, portio mea bona, salus mea sempiterna….

Christe Jesu, amabilis Domine, cur amavi, quare concupivi in omni vita mea quidquam praeter te Jesum Deum meum? Ubi eram quando tecum mente non eram? Jam ex hoc nunc, omnia desideria mea, incalescite et effluite in Dominum Jesum: currite, satis hactenus tardastis; properate quo pergitis; quaerite quem quaeritis. Jesu, qui non amat te anathema sit; qui non te amat amaritudinibus repleatur…. O dulcis Jesu, te amet, in te delectetur, te admiretur omnis sensus bonus tuae conveniens laudi.

---

5 St William of Paris.
6 *Meditationum*: Lib. I, Cap. xviii (Inter opp. S Augustini).

Deus cordis mei et pars mea, Christe Jesu, Deficiat cor meum spiritu suo, et vivas tu in me, et concalescat in spiritu meo vivus carbo amoris tui; ardeat jugiter in ara cordis mei, ferveat in medullis meis, flagret in absconditis animae meae; in die consummationis meae inveniar apud te.... Amen.[7]

I wanted to quote in Latin this wondrous prayer of St Augustine, so that those who understand Latin may say it every day to ask for the love of Jesus which we seek by Mary, His divine Mother.

ARTICLE II.

We belong to Jesus Christ and to Mary as their slaves.

68. *Second Truth.*—From what Jesus Christ is in regard to us, we must conclude, as the Apostle says, that we belong, not to ourselves, but entirely to Him as His members and His slaves,[8] whom He bought at an infinite price, the price of His Blood. Before Baptism we belonged to the devil as his slaves; and Baptism made us true slaves of Jesus Christ, who must live, work

---

7 (Translation of St Augustine's prayer)

Thou art Christ, my Holy Father, my tender God, my great King, my good Shepherd, my only Master, my best Helper, my most Beautiful and my Beloved, my living Bread, my Priest forever, my Leader to my country, my true Light, my holy Sweetness, my straight Way, my excellent Wisdom, my pure Simplicity, my peaceful Harmony, my entire Protection, my good Portion, my everlasting Salvation. Christ Jesus, sweet Lord, why have I ever loved, why in my whole life have I ever desired anything except Thee, Jesus my God? Where was I when I was not in spirit with Thee? Now, from this time forth, do ye, all my desires, grow hot, and flow out upon the Lord Jesus: run... ye have been tardy hitherto; hasten whither you are going; seek whom ye are seeking. O Jesus, may he who loves Thee not be anathema; may he who loves Thee not be filled with bitterness.

O sweet Jesus, may every good feeling that is fitted for Thy praise, love Thee, delight in Thee, admire Thee! God of my heart, and my portion, Christ Jesus, may my heart faint away in spirit, and mayest Thou be my life within me! May the live coal of Thy love grow hot within my spirit and break forth into a perfect fire; may it burn incessantly on the altar of my heart; may it glow in my innermost being; may it blaze in hidden recesses of my soul; and in the days of my consummation may I be found consummated with Thee! Amen.

8 1 Cor. vi, 19.

and die only to bear fruit for this God-Man,[9] to glorify Him in
our body, and to make Him reign in our soul, because we are
His conquest, the people of His acquisition and His heritage.
It is for the same reason that the Holy Ghost[10] compares us:
(1) to trees planted along the waters of grace in the field of the
Church, which must bear their fruit in due season; (2) to the
branches of a vine of which Jesus Christ is the stock, and which
must yield good grapes; (3) to a flock, of which Jesus Christ is
the Shepherd, and which is to increase and give milk; (4) to
good soil of which God is the husbandman, and in which the
seed is multiplied and brings forth thirty-fold, sixty-fold and
a hundred-fold. Jesus Christ cursed the barren fig tree[11] and
condemned the unprofitable servant who did not trade with
his talent.[12] All this proves that Jesus Christ wishes to receive
from our wretched selves some fruits, namely, our good works,
for they belong to Him alone: *creati in operibus bonis in Christo
Jesu….* "Created in good works in Christ Jesus".[13] These words
of the Holy Ghost show that Jesus Christ is the sole beginning
and must be the sole end of all our good works, and that we
must serve Him, not only as wage-servants, but as slaves of
love. I will explain what I mean.

69. There are two ways here on earth of belonging to another and depending on his authority, namely: simple service
and slavery; that is why we speak of a servant and of a slave.

By service, common among Christians, a man engages
himself to serve another for a certain period, at a fixed wage
or for some reward.

By slavery, a man is totally dependent on another for his
whole life and must serve his master without expecting any

---

9   Rom. vn, 4.
10 Cf. Ps. i, 3; John xv, 1 and x, 2; Mat. xiii, 3-8.
11 Mat. xxi, 19.
12 Mat. xxv, 24-30.
13 Eph. ii, 10.

wages or reward, like one of the beasts of the field, over which the master has the right of life and death.

70. Now there are three kinds of slavery:[14] natural slavery, forced slavery and voluntary slavery. All creatures are slaves of God in the first sense: *Domini est terra et plenitudo ejus* ...[15] The devils and the damned are slaves in the second sense; the saints and the just in the third. Voluntary slavery is the most perfect and the one which gives most glory to God, who beholdeth the heart,[16] who claims the heart[17] and calls Himself the God of the heart,[18] or of the loving will. And it is so, because by this slavery we choose God and His service before all things, even if this were not already an obligation of nature.

71. There is a total difference between a servant and a slave: (1) A servant does not give to his master all he is, all he has, and all he can acquire by himself or by others; but a slave gives himself whole and entire, all he has and all he can acquire to his master, without any exception. (2) A servant requires wages for the services which he renders to his master; but a slave can exact nothing, no matter what zeal, what industry, what energy he may put into his work. (3) A servant can leave his master whenever he pleases or at least when the time of his service expires; but the slave has no right to leave his master when he wishes. (4) A master has no right of life and death over a servant. Were he to kill him like one of his beasts of burden, he would commit murder. But the master of a slave has, by law, the right of life and death over him,[19] so

---

14 St Augustine: *Expositio cantici Magnificat*; St Thomas: *Summa*, p. 111, Qu. 48, Ad. 4.

15 Ps. xxiii, 1: "The earth is the Lord's and the fulness thereof."

16 I Kings xvi, 7.

17 Prov. xxiii, 26.

18 Ps. lxxii, 26.

19 Neither the natural nor the mosaic law, nor our human laws sanction this right of life and death. De Montfort only mentions a fact as it existed in uncivilised countries where such slavery was in force. Leaving aside the question of morality, he only wishes to give us an example of the complete dependence of which he speaks.

that he can sell him to whomsoever he wishes, or—without wishing to make a comparison—kill him as he would kill his horse. (5) Finally, a servant is in his master's service only for a time; a slave, for ever.

72. Among men there is nothing which makes one belong more to another than slavery; and so among Christians there is nothing which makes us belong more absolutely to Jesus Christ and His Holy Mother than voluntary slavery, after the example of Jesus Christ Himself, Who for love of us took the form of a slave: *Formam servi accipiens,*[20] and of the Blessed Virgin, who called herself the handmaid and slave of the Lord.[21] The Apostle calls himself, as by a title of honour, *Servus Christi....*[22] "The slave of Christ." Several times in Holy Scripture Christians are called *Servi Christi....* "Slaves of Christ." The word *servus,* as a great man has truly observed,[23] formerly meant nothing but slave, because there were no servants like those of the present day, masters being served either by slaves or by freed men. The Catechism of the Holy Council of Trent, to leave no doubt about our being slaves of Jesus Christ, expresses it by an unequivocal term, calling us *Mancipia Christi* ... "Slaves of Jesus Christ".[24] Granting this:

73. I say that we must belong to Jesus Christ and serve Him, not only as mercenary servants, but as loving slaves, who, as a result of great love, give and deliver themselves to serve Him as slaves, simply for the honour of belonging to

---

20 Phil, ii, 7.

21 Luke i, 38.

22 Rom i, 1; Gal. i, 10; Phil, i, 1; Tit. i, 1. The insistence on the part of the Apostles calling themselves "the slaves of Christ" shows that they did not believe that they were speaking in contradiction to the words of Christ: "I will not now call you slaves, but friends." John xv, 15... St Thomas Aquinas shows clearly how the disciples were slaves of Christ. *(In Evangelium Sti Joannis.)*

23 Henri-Marie Boudon, Archdeacon of Evreux, in his book *The Holy Slavery of the admirable Mother of God.*

24 Roman Catechism Part I, Chap. III.

Him. Before Baptism we were the slaves of the devil; Baptism made us slaves of Jesus Christ. Christians must be slaves either of the devil or of Jesus Christ.

74. What I say absolutely of Jesus Christ, I say relatively of Our Blessed Lady, to whom Jesus Christ—having chosen her as the inseparable companion of His life, His death, His glory and His power in heaven and on earth—has given by grace, relatively to His Majesty, the same rights and privileges that He possesses by nature. *Quidquid Deo convenit per naturam, Mariae convenit per gratiam....* "All that is fitting to God by nature is fitting to Mary by grace," say the Saints; so that, according to them, as Jesus and Mary have the same will and the same power, they have also the same subjects, servants and slaves.[25]

75. Following, therefore, the opinions of the Saints and of many great men, we can consider and make ourselves the loving slaves of Our Blessed Lady in order to be more perfectly the slaves of Jesus Christ.[26] The Blessed Virgin is the means which Our Lord took to come to us; she is also the means we must take to go to Him.[27] For she is not like other creatures, which, if we become attached to them, could rather lead us away from God than draw us to Him; the strongest inclination of Mary is to unite us to Jesus Christ, her Son, and the strongest inclination of the Son is that we should come to Him by His Blessed Mother. It pleases and honours Him, just as it would please and honour a king if, in order to become more perfectly his subject and his slave, one made oneself the slave of the queen. This is why the Holy Fathers, and St Bonaventure after them, declare that the Blessed Virgin is the way

---

25 St John Damascene *(Serrno in Dormitione B.M.).*

26 St Ildefonsus *(De virginitate perpetua B.M.).*

27 *Per ipsam Deus descendit ad terras, ut per ipsam homines ascendere mereantur ad caelos.* St Augustine *(Sermo in Nativitate Domini).* See also St Bonaventure *(Expositio in Luc.* Cap. I, no. 38) and Pius X (Encyclical *Ad diem ilium).*

which leads to Our Lord: *Via veniendi ad Christum est appropinquare ad illam.*[28]

76. Moreover if, as I have said,[29] the Blessed Virgin is the Queen and Sovereign of heaven and earth: *Imperio Dei omnia subjiciuntur et Virgo; ecce imperio Virginis omnia subjiciuntur et Deus*[30], as St Anselm, St Bernard, St Bernardine and St Bonaventure say, has she not then as many subjects and slaves as there are creatures? Is it not then reasonable that, among so many slaves of constraint there should be some slaves of love, who, of their own free will, and as slaves, should choose Mary for their Sovereign? What! men and demons shall have willing slaves and Mary shall have none? What! a king shall make it a point of honour that the queen, his consort, shall have slaves over whom she has right of life or death,[31] since the honour and power of the one is the honour and power of the other, and yet could we believe that Jesus Christ, who, as the best of sons, has shared His full power with His Blessed Mother, should take it ill that she should have slaves? Has He less respect and love for His Mother than Assuerus had for Esther and Solomon for Bethsabee? Who would dare say or even think it?

77. But where is my pen leading me? Why do I tarry here to prove something so evident? If people are unwilling to call themselves slaves of Mary, what does it matter? Let them become and call themselves slaves of Jesus Christ. This is the same as being slaves of Mary, for Jesus is the Fruit and the glory of Mary. This is what we do perfectly by the devotion of which we shall speak presently.

---

28 Psalter majus B.V., Ps. cxvii.
29 Cf. No. 38.
30 "All, even the B.V., are subject to the dominion of God; all, even God, are subject to the dominion of Mary."
31 Cf. footnote to No. 71.

ARTICLE III.

We must empty ourselves of what is evil in us.

78. *Third Truth.*—Our best actions are usually soiled and corrupted by the root of evil that is in us. When pure, clear water is put in a foul-smelling vessel, or wine into a cask that has been spoilt by another wine that was there before, both the clear water and the good wine are spoiled and easily contract the bad odour. In like manner, when God puts into the vessel of our soul, sullied by original and actual sin, the heavenly waters of His graces or the delicious wine of His love, His gifts are usually spoiled and tainted by the evil leaven and noxious dregs left in us by sin. Our acts, even of the most sublime virtues, feel the evil effects of it. It is therefore of the utmost importance that in seeking perfection, acquired only by union with Jesus Christ, we should rid ourselves of all that is evil in us; otherwise, Our Lord, who is infinitely pure and infinitely hates the slightest stain on our soul, will cast us from His presence and will not unite Himself to us.

79. To empty ourselves of self, firstly, we must become thoroughly aware, by the light of the Holy Ghost, of our corrupt nature, of our inability to do anything useful for salvation, of our weakness in all things, of our inconstancy at all times, of our unworthiness of any grace and of our ever-present sinfulness. The sin of our first parents has almost entirely spoiled, soured, puffed up and corrupted every one of us, just as leaven sours, raises and corrupts the dough in which it is placed. The actual sins we have committed, be they mortal or venial, even though forgiven, have increased our concupiscence, our weakness, our inconstancy, and our corruption and have left a sediment of evil in our soul.

Our bodies are so corrupt that they are called by the Holy Ghost bodies of sin,[32] conceived in sin, nourished in sin, and

---

32 Rom. vi, 6; Ps. l, 7.

capable of all sin; bodies subject to a thousand and one maladies, growing more corrupt from day to day, and engendering only disease, vermin and rottenness.

Our soul, united to our body, has become so carnal that it is called flesh: "All flesh had corrupted its way ".[33] All that we can call our own is pride and blindness of spirit, hardness of heart, weakness and inconstancy of soul, concupiscence, revolted passions, and sickness of body. By nature we are prouder than peacocks, we cleave to the earth more than toads, we are fouler than goats, more envious than serpents, greedier than pigs, fiercer than tigers, lazier than tortoises, weaker than reeds and more changeable than weathercocks. We have in us only sin and nothingness and merit only the anger of God and the eternity of hell.[34]

80. Is it surprising then that Our Lord has said that, whosoever wishes to follow him, must renounce himself and hate his own life, and that whosoever shall love his life shall lose it, and whosoever shall hate his life shall save it?[35] The Eternal Wisdom, who does not give commandments without reason, commands us to hate ourselves only because we so richly deserve to be hated. Nothing is so worthy of love as God, nothing is so worthy of hatred as ourselves.

81. Secondly, in order to rid ourselves of self, we must die daily to ourselves. That is to say, we must renounce the operations of the powers of our soul and of the senses of our body; we must see as if we saw not, hear as if we heard not and use the things of this world as if we did not use them.[36] This is what St Paul calls dying daily: *Quotidie morior.*[37] "Unless the

33 Gen. vi, 12.
34 De Montfort here speaks of our nothingness and incapability in the supernatural order without the assistance of grace. Thus he says further on, in No. 83, our nature is so corrupt that we cannot rely on our own good works to be united to God.
35 John xii, 25.
36 Cf. I Cor. vii, 29-30.
37 I Cor. xv, 31.

grain of wheat falling into the ground die, itself remaineth
alone arid does not bear any good fruit—" *Nisi granum fru-
menti, cadens in terram, mortuum fuerit, ipsum solum manet.*[38]
If we die not to ourselves, and if our most saintly devotions do
not bring us to this necessary and fruitful death, we shall bear
no good fruit, and our devotions will become useless to us, all
our good works will be tainted by self-love and self-will; and
God will hold in abomination the greatest sacrifices and the
best actions we may perform. Consequently, at our death, we
shall find ourselves destitute of virtues and merits and discover
that we have not even one spark of that pure love which is
granted only to souls that are dead to themselves and whose
life is hidden with Jesus Christ in God.[39]

82. Thirdly, among all the devotions to the Blessed Virgin, we must choose as the best and most sanctifying, that
which leads us most surely to this death to ourselves. For we
must not believe that all that glitters is gold, all that is sweet
is honey, and all which is easy to do and which is practised by
the greatest number is the most sanctifying. Just as there are
natural secrets enabling us to do certain natural things rapidly,
cheaply and easily, so in the order of grace, there are secrets
which enable us to perform supernatural works rapidly, sweet-
ly and easily: namely to rid ourselves of self, to fill ourselves
with God and to become perfect.

The devotion that I wish to disclose is one such secret of
grace, unknown to most Christians, known to but few of the
devout, practised and appreciated by fewer still. And now to
begin the disclosure of this devotion, here is a fourth truth
which is a sequel to the third.

---

38 John xii, 24-25.
39 Col. iii, 3.

ARTICLE IV.

We need a mediator with our Mediator Jesus Christ.

83. *Fourth Truth.*—It is more perfect, because more humble, not to approach God by ourselves, without taking a mediator. Our human nature, as I have just shown, is so corrupt, that if we rely on our own works, efforts and preparations in order to reach God and please Him, it is certain that our good works will be tainted, or they will be of little weight before God to induce Him to unite Himself to us and to hear us. For it is not without reason that God has given us mediators with His Majesty: He has seen our unworthiness and inability, He has had pity on us, and to give us access to His mercies, He has provided us with powerful intercessors with His Majesty; so that to neglect these mediators, and to approach His Holiness directly, and without any recommendation, is to fail in humility and in respect towards God, Who is so high and so holy. It would be showing less esteem for this King of kings than we would show for an earthly king or prince, whom we would not wish to approach without some friend to speak for us.

84. Our Lord is our Advocate and Mediator of redemption with God the Father. It is through Him that we ought to pray, with the whole Church triumphant and militant. It is by Him that we have access to God's Majesty, before whom we ought never to appear unless supported by and clothed with the merits of His Son; just as the young Jacob came before his father Isaac clothed in the skin of the kids to receive his blessing.

85. But do we not need a mediator with the Mediator Himself? Is our purity great enough to unite us directly and of ourselves to Him? Is He not God, in all respects equal to His Father, and consequently the Holy of Holies, just as worthy of respect as His Father? If, in His infinite charity, He became our surety and Mediator with God His Father, in order to appease Him and to pay our debts, are we on that account to have less respect and less fear for His Majesty and His Holiness?

Let us then say boldly with St Bernard[40] that we need a mediator with the Mediator Himself, and the divine Mary is the most capable of fulfilling this charitable office. It is by her that Jesus Christ came to us, and it is by her that we must go to Him. If we fear to approach directly Jesus Christ who is God, either because of His infinite greatness or because of our lowliness or our sins, let us implore without fear the aid and intercession of Mary, our Mother. She is kind, she is tender; there is nothing austere or hard in her, nothing too sublime or too dazzling. When we see her, we see our own human nature. She is not the sun, which by the brightness of its light could blind us because of our weakness. Rather is she sweet and gentle like the moon,[41] which receives the light of the sun and softens it in order to adapt it to our limited capacity. She is so loving that she rejects none who beg her intercession, however sinful they may be, for, as the Saints say, never has it been heard since the world existed, that anyone has had confident and persevering recourse to Our Blessed Lady, and was rejected. She is so powerful that her petitions have never been denied. She has but to appear before her Son, in order to pray to Him: at once He grants; at once He receives; He is lovingly conquered by the prayers of His dearest Mother who bore Him in her womb, and nursed Him at her breast.

86. All this is drawn from St Bernard and St Bonaventure, so that, according to them, we have three steps to mount when we go to God: the first, nearest to us and most suited,

---

40 *Serin, in Domin. infra octav. Assumptionis.* Most of this number is taken from St Bernard
41 Cant. vi, 9.

to our capacity, is Mary; the second is Jesus Christ; and the third is God the Father.[42] To go to Jesus, we must go to Mary: she is our mediatrix of intercession. To go to God the Father, we must go to Jesus: He is our Mediator of redemption. Now in the devotion which I shall expound hereafter, this order is perfectly observed.

ARTICLE V.

It is very difficult for us to preserve the graces and treasures received from God.

87. *Fifth Truth.*—It is very difficult, considering our weakness and frailty, to preserve in us the graces and treasures which we have received from God:—

1. Because we carry this treasure, more precious than heaven and earth, in fragile vessels: *habemus thesaurum istum in vasis fictilibus,*[43] i.e., in a corruptible body and in a weak and wavering soul, which a mere nothing disturbs and dejects.

88. 2. Because the devils, who are accomplished thieves, can surprise us unawares, to rob and strip us. Day and night they watch for a favourable time. They roam about incessantly seeking to devour us[44] and to snatch from us in one moment, by a sin, all the grace and merit we have taken years to acquire. Their malice, their experience, their cunning and their number ought to make us ever so much dread this misfortune, when we consider that people more full of grace than we, richer in virtue, more fully experienced and of higher sanctity have been unhappily surprised, robbed and pillaged. Ah! how many cedars of Lebanon, how many stars of the firmament have been known to fall miserably, and lose in but

---

42 See Leo XIII Encyclical *Octobri mense.*
43 1 Cor. iv, 7.
44 Cf. I Peter v, 8.

little time all their loftiness and all their brightness! What has brought about this strange reverse? It was not through want of grace, which is lacking to no one; it was through lack of humility. They thought themselves stronger, and more sufficient than they were; they thought themselves capable of keeping their treasures; they trusted and relied upon themselves; they thought their dwelling secure enough, and their coffers strong enough to safeguard the precious treasure of grace. And it was because of that imperceptible self-reliance (although it seemed to them that they were relying solely on the grace of God), that the most just Lord, leaving them to themselves, allowed them to be robbed. Alas! had they known the wonderful devotion that I shall presently unfold, they would have entrusted their treasure to the powerful and faithful Virgin, and she would have kept it for them as her own possession, even making of that trust an obligation in justice.

89. 3. It is difficult to persevere in righteousness because of the peculiar corruption of the world. The world is now so corrupt, that it seems almost inevitable that religious hearts be sullied,[45] if not by its mud, at least by its dust; so that it is a species of miracle that anyone can stand firm in the midst of this impetuous torrent without being carried away by it; in the midst of this stormy sea without being submerged or robbed by pirates and corsairs; in the midst of this pestilential air without being infected by it. It is the Virgin, singularly faithful, in whom the serpent has never had any part, who works this miracle for those who love her effectually.

---

45 St Leo the Great.

CHAPTER THREE.
CHOICE OF THE TRUE DEVOTION TO OUR BLESSED LADY.

90. These five truths having been laid down, it is more than ever necessary to choose rightly the *true* devotion to Our Blessed Lady, for now more than ever there are false devotions to her, which can easily be mistaken for true ones. The devil, like a counterfeiter and a crafty and experienced trickster, has already deceived and damned so many souls by means of false devotion to Our Lady that he makes daily use of his diabolical experience to damn many others, fooling them, lulling them to sleep in sin under the pretext of some prayers badly said or some exterior practices of devotion which he suggests to them. Just as a coiner normally counterfeits only gold and silver and but rarely any other metals, because they are not worth the trouble, even so the devil counterfeits not so much other devotions as those to Jesus and Mary—devotion to Holy Communion, devotion to Our Blessed Lady—for these are to other devotions what gold and silver are to other metals.

91. It is, then, very important, firstly, to know false devotions to Our Blessed Lady, in order to avoid them, and to know the true devotion, in order to embrace it. Secondly, to know which, among so many different practices of true devotion to Our Blessed Lady, is the most perfect, the most pleasing to her, the most glorious for God, and the most sanctifying for us, that we may cleave to it.

ARTICLE 1.

The characteristics of false devotions and of the true devotion to Our Lady.

A. False devotees and false devotions to Our Blessed Lady.

92. I find seven kinds of false devotees and false devotions to Our Lady, namely: 1. *critical* devotees; 2. *scrupulous* devotees; 3. *external* devotees; 4. *presumptuous* devotees; 5. *inconstant* devotees; 6. *hypocritical* devotees; 7. *self-interested* devotees.

1. Critical Devotees.

93. Critical devotees are, for the most part, proud scholars, strong-minded and self-sufficient people, who have in the main some devotion to the Blessed Virgin, but who criticise nearly all practices of devotion to her, which ordinary people perform simply and piously in honour of this good Mother, just because such practices are not according to their own fancy. They question all miracles and stories recorded by trustworthy authors or drawn from the chronicles of Religious Orders, which testify to the mercies and power of the most Blessed Virgin. They cannot bear to see simple and humble people on their knees before an altar or statue of Our Lady, perhaps at a street corner, offering prayers there to God; they even accuse them of idolatry, as if they were adoring the wood or the stone. They say that, for their part, they have no love for these exterior devotions, and are not so credulous as to believe all the stories and tales told of Our Blessed Lady. When you quote to them the wonderful praises offered by the Holy Fathers to Our Lady, they either reply that the Fathers were speaking as orators and were exaggerating, or they misinterpret their words.

Such false devotees and proud worldlings are much to be feared, and do infinite harm to devotion to the Blessed Virgin; and under pretext of destroying its abuses, they succeed only too well in driving people from it.

2. Scrupulous Devotees.

94. Scrupulous devotees are those who fear to dishonour the Son by honouring the Mother, to humiliate the one by exalting the other. They cannot bear that we should bestow on Our Lady the most just praises which the Holy Fathers have given her. It annoys them to see more people kneeling before the altar of the Blessed Virgin than before the Blessed Sacrament, as if one were contrary to the other, or as if those who pray to Our Blessed Lady did not pray to Jesus Christ through her. They do not want us to speak so often of her, to pray so often to her.

Here are some of their usual sayings: "What is the good of so many Rosaries, so many Confraternities, and so many external devotions to the Blessed Virgin? All this denotes much ignorance. It makes a mummery of our religion. I'd rather hear of those who are devout to Jesus Christ"; (yet they often pronounce His name without uncovering their heads: I say this by way of parenthesis). "We must have recourse to Jesus Christ; He is our only Mediator. We must preach Jesus Christ; this is solid devotion."

What they say is true in one sense; but because of the application they make of it, to hinder devotion to Our Lady, it is very dangerous and a subtle snare of the evil one, under pretext of a greater good; for never do we honour Jesus Christ more than when we honour more His Blessed Mother, because we honour her only in order to honour Him more perfectly, because we go to her only as the way which leads to the end we seek—Jesus Christ.

Jesus, or even equal to Him—that would be an intolerable
heresy; but in order to bless Jesus more perfectly, we must first
bless Mary. Let us say then with all those truly devoted to Our
Blessed Lady, in the face of these false and scrupulous devotees: "O Mary, blessed art thou among women, and blessed is
the fruit of thy womb, Jesus."

3. External Devotees.

96. External devotees are those who make their devotion
to Our Blessed Lady consist in exterior practices, who have
a taste for only the externals of devotion to her, because they
lack the interior spirit. They will say many Rosaries with great
haste, assist at several Masses without any attention, will take
part in her processions without devotion; they will join all her
Confraternities without amending their lives, without putting
any constraint on their evil passions and without imitating the
virtues of this most Holy Virgin. In their devotion they like
only what is apparent to the senses and have no taste for solidity. If they do not feel sensible sweetness in their practices, they
think they are doing nothing, they become unsettled, they give
everything up, or else they do everything by fits and starts. The
world is full of these external devotees; and there are no people
more critical of men of prayer, who, striving hard after interior devotion as the essential thing, do not neglect the exterior
composure which always accompanies true devotion.

4. Presumptuous Devotees.

97. Presumptuous devotees are sinners given up to their
evil passions, or lovers of the world, who, under the fair name

---

1 "Blessed art thou among women and blessed is the fruit of thy womb, Jesus."

of Christians and devotees of Our Blessed Lady, conceal their pride, avarice, impurities, drunkenness, anger, blaspheming, slandering, injustice, etc.; who sleep peacefully in their evil habits, without making much effort to correct themselves, under the pretext that they are devoted to the Blessed Virgin. They assure themselves that God will forgive them, that they will not die without confession and that they will not be damned, because they say the Rosary, because they fast on Saturdays, because they belong to the Confraternity of the Holy Rosary or of the Scapular, or belong to one of her Sodalities, or because they wear the little habit or the little chain of the Blessed Virgin, etc.

When you tell them that such devotion is just an illusion of the devil, and a most harmful presumption which may well ruin them, they refuse to believe you. They reply that God is good and merciful; that He has not made us to damn us, that no man is without sin; that they will not die without confession; that a good *peccavi* at death is quite enough. They say, moreover, that they are devoted to Our Blessed Lady, that they wear her scapular, that every day they say faithfully and humbly seven Our Fathers and seven Hail Marys in her honour; and that sometimes they say even the Rosary and the Office of Our Lady, besides fasting and so on. In proof of all they have said and to blind themselves still further they bring forward stories they have heard of or read—whether they be true or false matters little—stories relating how people who had died in mortal sin without confession were raised to life again to go to confession or how their soul had been miraculously retained in their bodies till confession; or how, because in their lifetime they said some prayers, or performed some practices of devotion to Our Lady, they obtained from God at the moment of death, through the mercy of the Blessed Virgin, contrition and pardon of their sins, and so have been saved. They accordingly hope that the same will happen to them.

98. Nothing in our Christian religion is so worthy of condemnation as this diabolical presumption, for how can we truthfully claim to love and honour the Blessed Virgin when by our sins we pitilessly wound, pierce, crucify and outrage her Son, Jesus Christ? If Mary made it a rule to save by her mercy this sort of people, she would be authorising crime and helping to crucify her Son. Who would ever dare think this?

99. I affirm that such abuse of devotion to Our Blessed Lady, which after devotion to Our Lord in the Blessed Sacrament, is the most holy and best devotion, is a most horrible sacrilege and, next to an unworthy Communion, the greatest and the least pardonable.

I admit that to be truly devout to Our Blessed Lady, it is not absolutely necessary to be so holy as to avoid every sin, though this is to be desired but at least it is necessary (note well what I am going to say): (1) to be sincerely resolved to avoid, at least, all mortal sin, which outrages the Mother as well as the Son; (2) to use violence to oneself to avoid sin; (3) to join her Confraternities, say the Rosary or other prayers, fast on Saturday, etc.

100. Such means are surprisingly effective in converting sinners, hardened though they might be, and if my reader were one of them, having already one foot in the abyss, I should advise him to do as I have said, but on condition that he practise such good works only to obtain from God, by the intercession of Our Lady, the grace of contrition and pardon for his sins, and grace to overcome his evil habits; and not that he might live peacefully in a state of sin, despite the warning voice of conscience, the example of Jesus Christ and the Saints, and the maxims of the holy Gospel.

5. Inconstant Devotees.

101. Inconstant devotees are those who are devout to Our Blessed Lady by fits and starts. At one moment they are fervent, at the next lukewarm. Sometimes they seem ready to do anything for her, and then, a little later, they are no longer the same. They begin by adopting all devotions to Our Lady; they join her Confraternities, then they do not observe the rules with fidelity. They change like the moon,[2] and with the moon Mary puts them beneath her feet, because they are inconstant and unworthy to be reckoned among the servants of this faithful Virgin, who share her fidelity and constancy. It were better not to burden oneself with so many prayers and practices of devotion, but rather to perform a few with love and fidelity in spite of the devil, the world and the flesh.

6. Hypocritical Devotees.

102. There are other false devotees of Our Lady, hypocritical ones, who cover their sins and evil habits under the mantle of this faithful Virgin so as to appear to their fellow men different from what they are.

7. Self-interested Devotees.

103. Again there are self-interested devotees, who have recourse to Our Lady only to win some lawsuit, to escape some danger, to be cured of some illness or for some other similar need; otherwise they would not think of her. All these are false devotees and are acceptable neither to God nor to His Holy Mother.

104. Let us beware then of joining the ranks of the critical devotees, who believe nothing and criticise everything; of the scrupulous devotees, who out of respect for Our Lord fear

---

2 The moon, because of its ever-changing phases, is taken as a symbol of inconstant souls. Cf. Eccl. xxvii, 12. See also St Bernard *(Sermo Super Signum Magnum)*.

to be too devoted to Our Lady; of the external devotees who make all their devotion consist wholly in outward practices; of the presumptuous devotees, who, under pretext of their false devotion to the Blessed Virgin, wallow in their sins; of the inconstant devotees, who by unsteadiness change their practices of devotion, or abandon them altogether at the slightest temptation; of the hypocritical devotees, who join Confraternities and wear badges of Our Lady, in order to appear good; and finally of the self-interested devotees who have recourse to Our Lady only to be delivered from the ills of the body or to obtain temporal goods.

B. True Devotion to Our Blessed Lady.

105. After having exposed and condemned the false devotions to the Blessed Virgin, I shall now briefly state in what the true devotion consists. It is: 1. *Interior;* 2. *Tender;* 3. *Holy;* 4. *Constant;* 5. *Disinterested.*

1. True Devotion is interior.

106. Firstly, true devotion to Our Lady is interior; that is, it comes from the spirit and the heart. It flows from the esteem in which we hold her, from the high opinion we have gained of her greatness, and from the love which we bear her.

2. True Devotion is tender.

107. Secondly, it is tender, that is to say, full of confidence in the Blessed Virgin, like a child's confidence in its loving mother. It causes us to have recourse to her in all our needs of body or soul with great simplicity, confidence and tenderness. We implore our Mother's help at all times, in all places, and in all things; in doubts, to be enlightened; in wanderings, to be set aright; in temptations, to be supported; in weaknesses, to be strengthened; in falls, to be lifted up; in discouragements, to be heartened; in scruples, to be freed from them; in crosses, trials, and disappointments of life, to be consoled. Finally, in all our ills of body or soul our habitual refuge is in Mary, and we have no fear of importuning her or of displeasing Jesus Christ.

3. True Devotion is holy.

108. Thirdly, true devotion to Our Lady is holy, that is to say, it leads us to avoid sin, and to imitate the virtues of the Blessed Virgin, particularly her deep humility, her lively faith, her blind obedience, her continual prayer, her universal mortification, her divine purity, her ardent charity, her heroic patience, her angelic meekness, and her divine wisdom. These are the ten principal virtues of the most Holy Virgin.

4. True Devotion is constant.

109. Fourthly, true devotion to Our Lady is constant. It strengthens us in doing good and prevails upon us not to abandon easily our practices of devotion. It makes us courageous in opposing the world with its fashions and its maxims, the flesh with its vexations and passions, and the devil with his temptations; so that a person truly devoted to Our Blessed Lady is not changeable, fretful, scrupulous or timid. This does not mean that such a one does not fall, and that his sensible feelings of devotion never change; but if he falls, he rises again, stretching out his hand to his good Mother. If he loses all savour and sensibility of devotion, he is not at all grieved; for the just and faithful devotee of Mary lives by the faith[3] of Jesus and Mary, and not by natural feeling.

5. True Devotion is disinterested.

110. Fifthly, true devotion to Our Lady is disinterested, which means that it prompts us to seek not ourselves but God

---

3 Heb. x, 38.

alone in His Blessed Mother. Those truly devout to Mary do not serve this august Queen for lucre or self-interest, nor for their own good, be it temporal or eternal, corporal or spiritual, but simply because she deserves to be served, and God alone in her. They love her not so much because she sends them favours, or because they expect any from her, but because she is lovable. This is why they love and serve her as faithfully in spiritual weariness and dryness as in spiritual sweetness and sensible fervour. They love her as much on Calvary as at the Wedding Feast of Cana. Oh! how pleasing and precious in the eyes of God and His Blessed Mother are such devotees of Our Blessed Lady, who have no self-seeking in their service of her. But how rare they are nowadays! To make them less rare I have taken pen in hand to put down on paper what I have taught with fruit, publicly and privately, in my missions for many years.

111. I have already said many things about the Blessed Virgin; but in my purpose of forming a true devotee of Mary and a true disciple of Jesus Christ, I have still more to say, and through ignorance, incapability or want of time I shall omit infinitely more.

112. Oh! how well my labour will have been spent if this little book, falling into the hands of a noble soul, born of God and of Mary, and not of blood, nor of the will of the flesh, nor of the will of man,[4] unfolds to him and inspires him, by the grace of the Holy Ghost, with the excellence and value of the true and solid devotion to Mary, which I shall presently describe. If I knew that my guilty blood could serve to engrave upon the heart of the reader the truths that I write in honour of my dear Mother and Sovereign Mistress, of whose children and slaves I am the least, I would use it instead of ink to trace these words, in the hope of finding noble souls, who

---

4 Cf. John i, 13.

by their fidelity to the practices I teach, will make amends to my dear Mother and Mistress for the losses which she has suffered through my ingratitude and infidelity.

113. More and more do I find myself inspired to believe and hope for all that is so deeply graven in my heart, and for which I have prayed to God for so many years, namely, that sooner or later the most Blessed Virgin will have more children, servants and slaves of love than ever;[5] and that, by this means, Jesus Christ, my dear Master, will reign more than ever in the hearts of men.

114. I clearly foresee that raging beasts will come in fury to tear to pieces with their diabolical teeth this little book and him whom the Holy Ghost has used to write it, or at least to bury it in the darkness and silence of a coffer, that it might not appear.[6] They will even attack and persecute those who read it and put it into practice. But what matter? So much the better! This vision encourages me and makes me hope for great success, that is to say, for a mighty legion of brave and valiant soldiers of Jesus and Mary, of both sexes, to fight the devil, the world, and corrupt nature in those more than ever perilous times that are to come!

"*Qui legit, intelligat.*[7] *Qui potest capere, capiat.*[8]

---

5   Notice the association of the terms "children" and "slaves." This is also found in the Catechism of the Council of Trent (Part I, Chap. III).

6   This prediction was literally verified. After De Montfort's death, his Missionaries were continually persecuted by the Jansenists for preaching this devotion. His treatise on the True Devotion was hidden away in a coffer during the French Revolution. It was discovered in 1842 by a Father of the Company of Mary among some old books in the library of the Mother House.

7   Mat. xxiv, 15: "He that readeth, let him understand."

8   Mat. xix, 12: "He that can take, let him take it."

ARTICLE II.

Practices of the true devotion to the Blessed Virgin.

A. Principal interior and exterior practices.

115. There are several *interior* practices of the true devotion to the Blessed Virgin. Here, in brief, are the principal ones: 1. To honour her as the worthy Mother of God, by the cult of hyperdulia: that is, to esteem and honour her more than all the other saints as the masterpiece of grace and the foremost after Jesus Christ, true God and true Man; 2. to meditate on her virtues, her privileges, and her actions; 3. to contemplate her greatness; 4. to offer to her acts of love, of praise, and of thanksgiving; 5. to invoke her with all our heart; 6. to offer and unite ourselves to her; 7. to perform all our actions with the intention of pleasing her; 8. to begin, continue and finish all our actions through her, in her, with her, and for her, in order to do them through Jesus Christ, in Jesus Christ, with Jesus Christ, and for Jesus Christ, our Last End. This last practice we will explain later.[9]

116. The true devotion to Our Lady has also several *exterior* practices among which these are the principal: 1. to enrol ourselves in her Confraternities, and enter her Sodalities; 2. to join the religious Congregations founded in her honour; 3. to proclaim her praises; 4. to give alms, to fast and practise interior and exterior mortifications in her honour; 5. to wear her livery, such as the rosary, the scapular, or the little chain; 6. to recite with attention, devotion and recollection either the Rosary, composed of fifteen decades of Hail Marys in honour of the fifteen principal mysteries of Jesus Christ; or else the Chaplet of five decades which is a third of the Rosary. It may be in honour of the five Joyful Mysteries, which are: the Annunciation,

---

9 Cf. Nos. 257-265.

the Visitation, the Birth of Our Lord, the Purification, and the Finding of the Child Jesus in the Temple. It may be in honour of the Sorrowful Mysteries: the Agony in the Garden, the Scourging at the Pillar, the Crowning with Thorns, the Carrying of the Cross, and the Crucifixion. Or it may be in honour of the five Glorious Mysteries: the Resurrection of Our Lord, His Ascension, the Coming of the Holy Ghost or Pentecost, the Assumption of Our Lady body and soul into heaven, and her Crowning by the three Persons of the Blessed Trinity. You may also say a Chaplet of six or seven decades in honour of the years which Our Lady is believed to have spent on this earth; or the Little Crown of the Blessed Virgin, consisting of three Our Fathers and twelve Hail Marys, in honour of her crown of twelve stars, i.e., her privileges; or the Office of Our Lady, so universally accepted and recited in the Church; or the Little Psalter composed in her honour by St Bonaventure, which is so tender and so devout that you cannot recite it without being touched by it; or fourteen Our Fathers and Hail Marys in honour of her fourteen joys; or some other prayers, hymns and canticles of the Church, such as the *Salve Regina,* the *Alma,* the *Ave Regina Caelorum,* or the *Regina Coeli,* according to the different liturgical seasons; or the *Ave Maris Stella,* the *O Gloriosa Domina,* the *Magnificat,* or some other devotional prayers found in all prayer books; 7. to sing hymns and have hymns sung in her honour; 8. to make genuflections or reverences to her a certain number of times, while saying, for example, sixty or a hundred times every morning, *Ave Maria, Virgo fidelis,* to obtain from God, by her intercession, fidelity to His graces throughout the day; and in the evening, the *Ave Maria, Mater Misericordiæ,* to ask through her pardon of God for sins committed during the day; 9. to take charge of her Confraternities, to decorate her altars, to crown and adorn her statues; 10. to carry her images or to have them carried in procession, and to wear one as a powerful protection against the Evil One; 11. to have her statues made or her name engraved, and placed in churches, or in houses, and on the gates and entries of towns, churches and houses; 12. to consecrate oneself to her in a special and solemn manner.

117. There are many other sanctifying practices of true devotion to the Blessed Virgin with which the Holy Ghost has inspired saintly souls. You can read them in detail in the *"Paradise opened to Philagia"* by Fr. Barry, of the Company of Jesus, wherein he has gathered a great number of devotions practised by the saints in honour of the Blessed Virgin; devotions which give wondrous help in the sanctification of souls, provided they are performed in the proper manner, that is: 1. with a good and right intention of pleasing God alone, of uniting oneself to Jesus Christ, our Last End, and of edifying one's neighbour; 2. with attention, avoiding voluntary distractions; 3. with devotion, avoiding haste and negligence; 4. with a modest, respectful and edifying attitude.

B. Choice of the Perfect Practice.

118. But having said all this, I unhesitatingly declare that, having read almost every book that treats of devotion to the Blessed Virgin, and having held familiar converse with the most saintly and learned people of recent times, I have never known or heard of a practice of devotion to Our Lady like the one I have in mind, which calls for more sacrifices for God, empties us more of self and self-love, keeps us more faithfully in grace and grace in us, unites us more perfectly and more easily to Jesus Christ; and which, finally, is more glorious to God, more sanctifying to the soul, and more useful to our neighbour.

119. As the essential part of this devotion consists in the interior state of soul which it must form, it will not be equally understood by everyone. Some—and by far the greater number—will stop at the exterior and go no further. Some— but few—will penetrate to the interior, but they will reach only the first degree. Who will reach the second? Who will reach the third? Finally, who will remain in it as in a permanent stage? He alone to whom the Spirit of Jesus Christ will reveal this secret. He, Himself, will lead the faithful soul to it, there to advance from virtue to virtue, from grace to grace, from light to light, reaching at last the transformation of self into Jesus Christ, and the plenitude of His age on earth, and His glory in heaven.

CHAPTER FOUR.

NATURE OF THE PERFECT DEVOTION TO THE BLESSED VIRGIN, OR THE PERFECT CONSECRATION TO JESUS CHRIST.

120. As our whole perfection consists in being conformed, united and consecrated to Jesus Christ, it follows that the most perfect of all devotions is clearly the one which conforms, unites and cones crates us most perfectly to Jesus Christ. Now, as Mary is of all creatures the most conformed to Jesus Christ, it follows that of all devotions, the one that most consecrates and conforms a soul to Our Lord is the devotion to the Blessed Virgin, His Holy Mother, and that the more a soul is consecrated to Mary, the more will it be cones crated to Jesus Christ.

It is for this reason that the perfect consecration to Jesus Christ is nothing else than a perfect and entire consecration of oneself to the Blessed Virgin, which is the devotion I teach. In other words, it is a perfect renewal of the vows and promises of Baptism.

ARTICLE I.

A perfect and entire consecration of ourselves to the Blessed Virgin.

121. This devotion consists, then, in giving oneself entirely to the Blessed Virgin, in order to belong entirely to Jesus Christ through her.[1] We must give her 1. our body, with all its senses and members; 2. our soul, with all its powers; 3. our exterior possessions, present and future; 4. our interior

---

1 St John Damascene *(Sermo in Dormitione B. V.)* ... "We consecrate to thee our mind, our soul, our body and our whole selves."

and spiritual possessions, that is, our merits, virtues and good works past, present and future; in a word, all that we have in the order of nature and in the order of grace, and all that we may possess in the future in the order of nature, of grace and of glory; this we give without reserve of a farthing, a hair or the least good work; we give for all eternity and without expectation or hope of any other reward for our offering and service than the honour of belonging to Jesus Christ through her and in her, even though that good Mistress were not—as she always is—the most generous and thankful of creatures.

122. Here we must note that two things are to be considered in our good works, namely, satisfaction and merit; in other words, their satisfactory or impetratory value, and their meritorious value. The satisfactory or impetratory value of a good work is the good action inasmuch as it satisfies for the punishment due to sin or obtains a new grace; the meritorious value or the merit is the good action inasmuch as it merits grace and eternal glory. Now, by this consecration of ourselves to the Blessed Virgin, we give her all satisfactory, impetratory and meritorious value, in other words, the satisfaction and the merits of all our good works. We give her our merits, graces and virtues not that she might give them to others (for our merits, graces and virtues are, strictly speaking, incommunicable; only Jesus Christ, in making Himself our surety with His Father, was able to communicate to us His merits), but that she may keep, increase and beautify them for us, as we shall explain later.[2] We give her our satisfactions that she may communicate them to whomsoever she pleases, and for the greater glory of God.

123. 1. It follows from this, that by this devotion we give to Jesus Christ, in the most perfect manner—since it is through the hands of Mary—all that we can give Him, and far more

2 Cf. No. 146.

than is given by other devotions, which present Him with only part of our time, of our good works, or of our satisfactions and mortifications. By this devotion everything is given and consecrated, even the right to dispose of one's interior goods, and the satisfaction acquired by daily good works—a thing which is done in no Religious Congregation. In Religious Congregations we give God our material belongings by the vow of poverty, our bodily goods by the vow of chastity, our own will by the vow of obedience, and sometimes our freedom of movement by the vow of enclosure. But by these vows we do not give Him the liberty or right we possess to dispose of the value of our good works, nor do we strip ourselves, as much as we can, of that which the Christian considers his most precious and dearest belongings, namely, his merits and satisfactions.

124. 2. From this it follows that anyone who has thus willingly consecrated and sacrificed himself to Jesus through Mary can no longer dispose of the value of any of his good actions. All he suffers, all he thinks, all the good he says and does, belongs to Mary, so that she may dispose of it according to the will of her Son, and for His greater glory. This dependence however in no way prejudices the obligations of one's present or future state of life; as for example, the obligations of a priest, who, by his office or otherwise, has to apply the satisfactory and impetratory value of the Holy Mass to some particular person; for this offering is made only according to the order established, by God and the duties of our state in life.

125. 3. It follows also that we consecrate our selves at one and the same time to the Blessed Virgin and to Jesus Christ; to the Blessed Virgin, as to the perfect means that Jesus Christ chose to unite Himself to us, and to unite us to Him; and to Our Lord, as to our final end, to whom we owe all that we are, as to our Redeemer and our God.

ARTICLE II.

A perfect renewal of the vows of Holy Baptism.

126. I have said[3] that this devotion may rightly be called a perfect renewal of the vows or promises of Holy Baptism.

Every Christian before Baptism was the slave of the devil, because he belonged to him. In Baptism, he has, either by his own mouth or by his sponsors, solemnly renounced Satan, his pomps and his works, and taken Jesus Christ as his Master and Sovereign Lord, to depend upon Him as a slave of love. We do the same thing by this present devotion; we renounce (as is expressed in the Act of Consecration) the devil, the world, sin and self; and we give ourselves entirely to Jesus Christ through the hands of Mary. We do even more, for, in Baptism, we ordinarily speak by the mouth of another, namely, by our godfather and godmother—we give ourselves to Jesus Christ by proxy; but in this devotion, we do so by ourselves, voluntarily, and with knowledge of what is involved.

In holy Baptism, we do not give ourselves to Jesus Christ through the hands of Mary, at least not explicitly, nor do we give Him the value of our good actions. We remain, after Baptism, quite free to apply it to whom we wish or to keep it for ourselves. But by this devotion we give ourselves explicitly to Jesus Christ through the hands of Mary, and consecrate to Him the value of all our actions.

127. Man, says St Thomas, vows in holy Baptism to renounce the devil and all his pomps: *In Baptismo vovent homines abrenuntiare diabolo et pompis ejus.* This vow, says St Augustine, is the greatest and the most indispensable: *votum maximum nostrum quo vovimus nos Christo esse mansuros* (Epistola 59 ad Paulin). Canonists say the same: *Praecipuum*

---

3 Cf. No. 120.

votum est quod in Baptismate facimus.[4] Yet who keeps this great vow? Who faithfully fulfils the promises of holy Baptism? Do not almost all Christians swerve from the loyalty which they promised Jesus Christ in their Baptism? And whence can this universal disloyalty come if not from habitual forgetfulness of the promises and obligations of holy Baptism, and from the fact that hardly anyone makes a personal ratification of this contract of alliance made with God through our god-parents.

128. This is so true that the Council of Sens, convened by order of King Louis the Debonnaire to remedy the great disorders prevailing among Christians, judged that the principal cause of this corruption of heart was habitual forgetfulness and ignorance of the obligations of Baptism, nor could it find a better means of curing so great an evil than to urge Christians to renew the vows and promises of Baptism.

129. The Catechism of the Council of Trent, faithful interpreter of that Holy Council, exhorts parish priests to do the same thing, and to induce the people to recall to mind and to believe that they are bound and consecrated to Our Lord Jesus Christ, as slaves to their Redeemer and Lord. These are its words: *Parochus fidelem populum ad earn rationem cohortabitur ut sciat aequissimum esse ... nos ipsos, non secus ac mancipia Redemptori nostro et Domino in perpetuum addicere et consecrate* (Cat. Conc. Trid. p. I, c. 3).[5]

130. Now if the Councils, the Fathers, and experience itself show us that the best way to remedy the disloyalty of Christians is to remind them of the obligations of their Baptism, and to make them renew the vows they then made, is it not reasonable that we should do it now in a perfect manner by this devotion and consecration to Our Lord through His

---

4 "The principal vow is the one we make in Baptism."
5 "The Parish Priest shall exhort the faithful so that they may know that it is most just... that they should devote and consecrate themselves to their Lord and Redeemer as His very slaves."

Blessed Mother? I say in a perfect manner for by it we make use of the most perfect means of consecrating ourselves to Jesus Christ—the most Blessed Virgin.

Answers to some objections.

131. It cannot be objected that this devotion is new or unimportant; it is not new, for the Councils, the Fathers, and many authors both ancient and modern, speak of this consecration to Our Lord, or renewal of the vows of holy Baptism, as something practised from ancient times, and which they counsel to all the faithful; it is not unimportant, seeing that the principal source of all moral disorders, and consequently of the eternal perdition of Christians, comes from forgetfulness of and unconcern towards this practice.

132. Some might object that because this devotion makes us give Our Lord through the hands of the Blessed Virgin all our good works, prayers, mortifications and almsdeeds, it renders us unable to help the souls of our parents, friends and benefactors.

To this I reply: firstly, that it is unbelievable that our friends, relatives or benefactors should suffer any loss from the fact that we are devoted and consecrated without reserve to the service of Our Lord and His Blessed Mother. It would be an insult to the power and goodness of Jesus and Mary, who know well how to assist our relatives, friends and benefactors, either out of our own little spiritual store or by other means.

Secondly, this practice does not prevent us from praying for others, whether dead or living, even though the application of our good works depends on the will of Our Blessed Lady. It is, on the contrary, something which will make us pray with greater confidence; just as a rich person, who, to honour his prince, has given him everything he possessed, would with greater confidence ask his help for one of his friends who begged assistance. Indeed, such an opportunity of showing gratitude to a person who had stripped himself to enrich him and beggared himself to honour him, would surely be pleasing to the prince. The same can be said of Our Lord and the Blessed Virgin—they will never allow themselves to be outdone in gratitude.

133. Some may perhaps say: if I give to Our Lady the full value of my actions to apply it to whom she wills, I shall perhaps have to suffer a long time in Purgatory.

This objection, springing from self-love and from ignorance of the generosity of God and His Holy Mother, destroys itself. A fervent and generous soul who values God's interests more than his own, who gives God all he has without reserve, till he can give no more, *non plus ultra,* who desires only the glory and reign of Jesus Christ through His Holy Mother, and to gain which he sacrifices himself utterly; will this generous and unselfish soul, I say, be punished in the next world for having been more generous and unselfish than others? Very far from it: it is towards just such a soul, as we shall see later, that Our Lord and His Blessed Mother show themselves most generous in this world and in the world to come, in the order of nature, of grace and of glory.

134. We must now consider as briefly as possible: 1. The *motives* which ought to recommend this devotion to us; 2. The *wondrous effects* it produces in faithful souls; and 3. The *practices* of this devotion.

CHAPTER FIVE.

THE MOTIVES WHICH SHOULD RECOMMEND THIS DEVOTION TO US.

ARTICLE I.

By this devotion we give ourselves up entirely to the service of God.

135. *First motive, which shows us the excellence of this conse-cration of oneself to Jesus Christ by the hands of Mary.*

If we can conceive no position on earth higher than that of being in the service of God, and if the least servant of God, is richer, more powerful and more noble than all the kings and emperors on earth—unless they also are the servants of God—what then must be the riches, the power and the dig-nity of the faithful and perfect servant of God, who is devoted to His service entirely, without reserve, and as much as in him lies? Such is the faithful and loving slave of Jesus in Mary, who has surrendered himself entirely to the service of the King of kings, by the hands of His Blessed Mother, and has reserved nothing for himself; he is worth more than all the gold of the world and the beauties of the heavens.

136. Other congregations, associations and confrater-nities set up in honour of Our Lord and Our Blessed Lady and which do so much good work throughout Christendom, do not make us give up everything without reserve, for they prescribe only certain acts and practices to their members as fulfilment of their obligations, leaving them free to dispose of all other actions and moments of their life. But this devo-tion makes us give Jesus and Mary, without reserve, all our thoughts, words, actions and sufferings and every moment of our lives. In this fashion, be we waking or sleeping, eating or drinking, performing mighty works or the very humblest, it can be always truly said that whatever we do—whether we think of it or not—is done for Jesus and Mary, by virtue of our offering; and this holds true unless we have expressly retracted it. How consoling this is!

137. Moreover, as I have already said,[1] there is no practice other than this by which we easily rid ourselves of a certain sense of ownership which slips imperceptibly into even our best actions. This special grace our loving Jesus grants us in rewards for the heroic and unselfish act of handing over to Him through the hands of Mary the full value of all our good works. If, even in this world, He gives a hundredfold to those who for love of Him leave exterior, temporal and perishable things,[2] what will be the hundredfold He will give to those . who sacrifice for Him even their interior and spiritual goods!

138. Jesus, our dearest friend, gave Himself to us without reserve, body and soul, virtues, graces and merits: *Se toto totum me comparavit*, says St Bernard. "He has bought me entirely by giving Himself entirely." Is it not simple justice and gratitude that we should give Him all we possibly can? He was the first to be generous, let us be generous in return, and during our life, at our death and throughout eternity we shall find Him still more generous: *Cum liberali liberalis erit.*[3]

ARTICLE II.

By this devotion we imitate the example given us by Jesus Christ and by God Himself; and we practise humility.

139. *Second motive, which shows us that it is just in itself and advantageous to our souls to consecrate ourselves entirely to*

---

1 Cf. No. 110.
2 Mat. xix, 29.
3 "With the liberal he will be liberal."

*the Most Blessed Virgin by this practice, in order to belong more
perfectly to Jesus Christ.*

This good Master did not disdain to shut Himself up in the
womb of the Blessed Virgin, like a captive and a loving slave,
and to be subject and obedient to her for thirty years. It is here,
I repeat, that the human mind is lost, when it ponders serious-
ly on this conduct of the Incarnate Wisdom, Who, although
He could have done so, willed to give Himself not directly to
mankind, but rather through the Most Blessed Virgin; Who
willed to come on this earth, not as a man at the flower of His
age, completely independent, but as a poor little babe, dependent on the care and support of His Blessed Mother. This Infinite Wisdom, Who had a boundless desire to glorify God, His
Father, and to save mankind, found no shorter or more perfect
means to accomplish this than to submit Himself in all things
to the most Blessed Virgin; not only during the first eight, ten
or fifteen years of His life, like other children, but for thirty
years. He gave more "glory to God His Father during all that
time of submission to and dependence on Our Blessed Lady,
than He would have given Him, had He passed those thirty
years in working miracles, in preaching to the whole world, in
converting all men; had it been otherwise He would have done
so. Oh! oh! how greatly do we glorify God, when, in imitation
of Jesus, we submit ourselves to Mary!

With such an evident and such a well-known example before us, are we so foolish as to believe that we can find a more
perfect and a shorter means of glorifying God than submitting
ourselves to Mary, after the example of her Son?

140. Let us recall here as proof of the dependence we
should have on Our Blessed Lady, what I have said above,[4]
when I brought forward the examples which the Father, the
Son, and the Holy Ghost give us concerning the dependence

---

4 Cf. 14-39.

which we should have on her. The Father gave and still gives His Son only through her; raises for Himself children only through her, communicates His graces only through her. God the Son has been formed for Mankind in general only through her; He is formed daily and engendered only through her in union with the Holy Ghost, and only through her does He communicate His merits and virtues. The Holy Ghost formed Jesus Christ only through her, forms the members of Christ's Mystical Body and dispenses His gifts and favours only through her. Having so many and such pressing examples of the Blessed Trinity before us, how can we, without an extremity of blindness, fail to make use of Mary, fail to consecrate ourselves to her and to depend on her to go to God and sacrifice ourselves to Him?

141. Here are a few Latin passages from the Fathers which I have chosen to prove what I have just said: *Duo filii Mariae sunt, homo Deus et homo purus; unius corporaliter, et alterius spiritualiter Mater est Maria.* (St Bonaventure and Origen).[5]

Haec est voluntas Dei, qui totum nos voluit habere per Mariam; ac proinde, si quid spei, si quid gratiae, si quid salutis, ab ea noverimus redundare. (St Bernard).[6]

Omnia dona, virtutes, gratiae ipsius Spiritus Sancti, quibus vult, et quando vult, quomodo vult, quantum vult, per ipsius manus administrantur. (St Bernardine).[7]

Quia indignus eras cui daretur, datum est Mariae, ut per earn acciperes quidquid haberes. (St Bernard).[8]

5   " Mary has two sons; the one a God-man, the other a mere man; of the one she is the mother corporally; of the other spiritually." *(Speculum B.V.M.)*
6   "This is the will of God, Who willed that we should have all things through Mary. If then there is in us any hope, or grace, or gift of salvation, let us know that it comes to us through her." *(De Aquaeductu. No. 6).*
7   "All the gifts, virtues and graces of the Holy Ghost Himself are distributed by the hands of Mary to whom she wills, when she wills, as she wills, and in the measure she wills."
8   "As you were not worthy that anything should be given to you, all graces were given to Mary that through her you should receive whatever you are to have." *(Sermo in Nativ. Domini).*

142. St Bernard tells us that God, seeing we are unworthy to receive His graces immediately from His hands, gives them to Mary, so that we might have through her all that He wishes to give us. Moreover, He finds His glory in receiving by the hands of Mary the gratitude, respect and love we owe in return for His benefits. It is but just therefore that we should imitate His conduct "in order," as St Bernard says,[9] "that grace might return to its author, by the same channel through which it came." *Ut eodem alveo ad largitorem gratia redeat quo fluxit.*

That is what we do by our devotion. We offer and consecrate all we are and all we have to the Blessed Virgin, in order that Our Lord may receive through her mediation the glory and gratitude that we owe Him. We acknowledge ourselves unworthy and unfit to approach His Infinite Majesty by ourselves; and therefore we make use of the intercession of the most Blessed Virgin.

143. Moreover, this devotion is a practice of deep humility, a virtue which God loves above all the other virtues. A soul that exalts itself lowers God; a soul that humbles itself exalts God. "God resists the proud and gives His grace to the humble."[10] If you humble yourself, believing yourself unworthy to appear before Him and to approach Him, He descends and lowers Himself to come to you, to take His delight in you and to exalt you in spite of yourself. But, on the contrary, if you approach God rashly, using no mediator, He flies from you and you cannot reach Him.[11] Oh! Oh! how He loves humility of heart! It is to such humility that the practice of this devotion leads us, for it teaches us never to approach Our Lord directly, however gentle and merciful He may be, but to make use always of the intercession of the Most Blessed

---

9   De Aquaeductu. No. 18.
10 James iv, 6.
11 Si Aug. *(De Ascensione Domini).*

Virgin, whether it be to appear before Him, to speak to Him, to approach Him, to offer Him something or to unite and consecrate ourselves to Him.

ARTICLE III.

This devotion obtains for us the favours of Our Lady.

1. Mary gives herself to her slave of love.

144. *Third Motive.*—The most Blessed Virgin, who is a Mother of gentleness and mercy and who never allows herself to be outdone in love and liberality, seeing that a soul gives itself entirely to her to honour and serve her, stripping itself of all it holds dear in order to adorn her, gives herself completely and in an ineffable manner to him who gives all to her. She causes him to be engulfed in the abyss of her graces; she adorns him with her merits; she upholds him with her power; she enlightens him with her radiance; she inflames him with her love; she communicates to him her virtues, her humility, her faith, her purity, etc.; she makes herself his surety, his supplement, and his very all with Jesus. In short, as he who is consecrated to Mary is all her own, so is she all his own; so that we can say of this perfect servant and child[12] of Mary what St John the Evangelist said of himself, that he took the Blessed Virgin unto his own: *Accepit earn discipulus in sua.*[13]

145. This produces in his soul, if he be faithful, a great distrust, contempt and hatred of self, together with great confidence and self-abandonment to the Blessed Virgin his good Mistress. He no longer, as before, relies on his own dispositions, intentions, merits, virtues and good works, for as he has sacrificed them completely to Jesus through this gentle

---

12 Cf. No. 113.
13 John xix, 27.

Mother, he has now but one store-house where all his treasures are laid up; it is no longer in himself, for his treasury is Mary.

This makes him approach Our Lord without servile or scrupulous fear and pray to Him with much confidence; it makes him share the feelings of the devout and learned Abbot Rupert, who, alluding to the victory that Jacob gained over the angel,[14] spoke to Our Blessed Lady these beautiful words: "O Mary, my princess, Immaculate Mother of the Incarnate God, Jesus Christ, I desire to wrestle with this Man, the Divine Word, armed not with my own merits but with thine." *O Domina, Dei Genitrix, Maria, et incorrupta Mater Dei et hominis, non meis sed tuis armatus mentis, cum isto Viro, scilicet Verbo Dei, luctari cupio* (Rup. prolog. in Cantic.) Oh! how strong and mighty are we with Jesus Christ when armed with the merits and intercession of the worthy Mother of God, who, as St Augustine said, has lovingly vanquished the Most High!

2. Mary purifies our good works, beautifies them and makes them acceptable to her Son.

146. Since by this devotion we give Our Lord, by the hands of His holy Mother, all our good works, this loving Mistress cleanses them and beautifies them, and makes them acceptable to her Son.

(i) She purifies them of all that stain of self-love and imperceptible attachment to creatures which slips unnoticed into even our best actions. Immediately they have reached her most pure and fruitful hands, these same hands, which have never known stain or idleness and which purify all they touch, remove from the gift made to her all that is tainted and imperfect.

14 Gen. xxxii, 24.

147. (ii) She beautifies them by adorning them with her own merits and virtues. It is as if a peasant, desirous of gaining the friendship and benevolence of a king, were to go to the queen and present her with an apple—his whole revenue—that she might offer it to the king. The queen, having accepted the little offering from the peasant, would place the apple on a large and beautiful dish of gold, and thus present it to the king, on behalf of the peasant. Then the apple, although unworthy of itself to be offered to the king, would become a present worthy of his Majesty, because of the dish of gold on which it lies and because of the person who presented it.

148. (iii) She presents our good works to Jesus Christ; for she does not keep for herself, as if she were the last end, anything that is offered to her; she forwards all faithfully to Jesus. If we give to her, we necessarily give to Jesus. If we praise and glorify her, she at once praises and glorifies Jesus. As of old, when St Elizabeth praised her, so now, when we praise and bless her, she sings: *Magnificat anima mea Dominum.*[15]

149. (iv) However poor and wretched a present our good works may be for the Holy of Holies and King of Kings, she makes them acceptable to Jesus. When, by ourselves and relying on our own merits and dispositions, we present something to Jesus, He examines it and frequently rejects it because of stains of self-love, just as He once rejected the sacrifices of the Jews, full as they were of self-will. But when we present Him anything by the pure and virginal hands of His Wellbeloved, we take Him by His weak point, if I can make use of such an expression. He considers not so much the gift as the gentle Mother who presents it. He notices not so much whence it comes as by whom it comes. Thus Mary, never rejected, always well received by her Son, induces Him to receive favourably anything she offers, be it great or small. It is

---

15 Luke i, 46. "My soul doth magnify the Lord."

sufficient that Mary presents something for Jesus to receive and accept it. This is the sound advice given by St Bernard to those whom he was leading to perfection: "When you wish to offer something to God, unless you want to be rejected, take care to offer it through the most pleasing and worthy hands of Mary."—*Modicum quid offerre desideras, manibus Mariae offerendum tradere cura, si non vis sustinere repulsam;* (St Bernard, Lib. de Aquaed.)

150. Does not nature itself, as we have seen,[16] suggest this mode of procedure to the little of this world with regard to the great? Why should not grace lead us to do the same thing with regard to God, who is infinitely exalted above us, and before whom we are less than atoms, especially as we have an advocate so powerful that she is never refused, so industrious that she knows all the secrets for gaining the heart of God, so kind and loving that she repels no one, however little and wicked he might be.

I shall speak, further on,[17] of the true figure of these truths in the story of Jacob and Rebecca.

ARTICLE IV.

This devotion is an excellent means of giving greater glory to God.

151. *Fourth motive.* This devotion, faithfully practised, is an excellent means of making sure that the value of all our good works shall be used for the greater glory of God. Scarcely anyone works for that noble end (although we are under an obligation to do so), either because we do not know where God's greater glory is to be found, or because we do not desire it. But as Our Blessed Lady to whom we cede the value and merit of

---

16 Cf. No. 147.
17 Cf. Chapter vi.

our good actions, knows perfectly where God's greater glory is to be found and acts only for that end, a perfect servant of this good Mistress, totally consecrated to her, as we have said, can boldly affirm that the value of all his actions, thoughts and words is used for the greater glory of God, unless he expressly revokes his offering. Is there anything more consoling for one who loves God purely and without self-interest, and sets God's glory and interests above his own?

ARTICLE V.

This devotion leads to union with Our Lord.

152. *Fifth motive.* This devotion is an *easy, short, perfect* and *sure* way of attaining union with Our Lord, in which Christian perfection consists.

1. This devotion is an easy way.

It is an *easy* way; it is the path which Jesus Christ opened in coming to us and in which there lies no obstacle in reaching Him. It is quite true that we can attain to divine union by other paths, but by many more crosses and strange deaths and at the cost of many difficulties that we shall not easily overcome. We would have to pass through dark night, through strange struggles and agonies, over precipitous mountains, among painful thorns and through terrifying deserts. But along the path which is Mary we walk gently and peacefully. Here, it is true, we have hard battles to fight and great difficulties to overcome; but this loving Mother and Mistress makes herself so near, so present to her faithful servants, to lighten their darkness, to illuminate them in their doubts, to strengthen them in their fears, to uphold them in battle and in difficulty that truly, in comparison with other ways, this virginal path in the quest for Christ is a way of roses and honey. There have been some saints, though they be but few, such as St Ephrem, St John Damascene, St Bernard, St Bernardine, St Bonaventure, St Francis de Sales, and others, who have taken this sweet path to go to Jesus Christ, because the Holy Ghost, faithful Spouse of Mary, by a special grace revealed it to them. But the other Saints, who are the greater number, although they all had devotion to Our Blessed Lady, did not enter, or but very slightly entered, upon this way; that is why they had to pass through harder and more dangerous trials.

153. How is it then, a servant of Mary might ask me, that faithful servants of this good Mother have so much to suffer, more indeed, than those who are less devoted to her? They are contradicted, persecuted, calumniated, people cannot bear them; or else, they live in interior darkness and spiritual deserts where there is not the least drop of heavenly dew. If this devotion to the Blessed Virgin renders easier the path to Jesus Christ, how is it that they are the most afflicted?

154. I reply that it is quite true that the most faithful servants of the Blessed Virgin, being her greatest favourites, receive from her the greatest graces and favours from heaven, which are crosses. But I maintain that it is also these servants of Mary who bear these crosses with more facility, more merit and more glory. That which would check the progress of another a thousand times over, or perhaps bring about his fall, does not hinder them at all, but rather makes them advance; for this good Mother filled with the grace and unction of the Holy Ghost, steeps all these crosses she carves for them, in the sugar of her maternal sweetness and the unction of pure love, so that they swallow them cheerfully like sweetened nuts, though in themselves they may be very bitter. And I think that anyone who wishes to be devout and to live piously in Jesus Christ, and consequently to suffer persecution, and carry his cross daily,[18] will never carry heavy crosses, or carry them joyfully and perseveringly, without a tender devotion to Our Lady, who is the sweetness of the cross; just as, without great efforts which cannot last, one could not eat unripened nuts which are not preserved in sugar.

2. This devotion is a short way.

155. This devotion to the Blessed Virgin is a *short* way to find Jesus Christ, either because we do not wander, or because, as I have just said, we walk in it with greater joy and facility, and consequently with more promptitude. We advance more in a short period of submission to and dependence on Mary than in whole years of self-love and self-reliance. For *the obedient man* submitted to the divine Mary *will sing* of signal *victories* over all his enemies.[19] True, they will strive to hinder his advance, to force him back or bring about his fall; but with the support, the help and the guidance of Mary, he will, without falling, without drawing back, and even without delay, advance with giant strides to Jesus Christ along that same way by which—as it is written[20]—Jesus came to us with giant strides and in but a short time.

156. Why, think you, did Jesus Christ live so few years on earth and yet spend nearly all of them in submission and obedience to His Mother? Ah! it is that being made perfect in a short space, He fulfilled a long time,[21] a longer time than Adam whose losses He had come to make good, though Adam lived for nine hundred years. Jesus Christ lived a long time because in obedience to God His Father He lived in submission to His Mother and closely united with her. For, (i) he who honours his mother, says the Holy Ghost, is like a man

---

18   2 Tim. iii, 12.
19   Prov. xxi, 28
20   Ps. xviii, 6.
21   Wisdom iv, 13.

that layeth up treasure; that is to say, he who honours Mary, his Mother, even to submitting himself to her and obeying her in all things, will soon become exceedingly rich, because he is every day laying up treasure by the secret of this philosopher's stone: *Qui honorat matrem, quasi qui thesaurizat.*[22] (ii) Because, according to a mystical interpretation of these words of the Holy Ghost: *Senectus mea in misericordia uberi.*—"My old age is in the mercy of the bosom,"[23] it is in the womb of Mary which has *encompassed and engendered a perfect man,*[24] *and which was able to contain Him whom the universe can neither contain nor comprehend,*[25] it is, I say, in the womb of Mary that they who are youthful become elders in light, in holiness, in experience and in wisdom; and that we attain in a short time to the fulness of the age of Jesus Christ.

3. This devotion is a perfect way.

157. This devotion to Our Blessed Lady is a *perfect* way to go to Christ and to unite ourselves to Him, for the divine Mary is the most perfect and the most holy of mere creatures, and because Jesus Christ, who came to us in a perfect manner, chose no other path for His great and wondrous journey. The Most High, the Incomprehensible, the Inaccessible, He who Is, willed to come to us, little worms of the earth, who are nothing. How was this done?

The Most High came down to us through the humble Mary, divinely, perfectly, losing nothing of His Divinity and Holiness; and through Mary, perfectly, divinely, fearing nothing, we little ones must ascend to the Most High.

The Incomprehensible allowed Himself to be comprehended and perfectly contained by the humble little Mary,

22 Eccli. iii, 5.
23 Ps. xci, 11.
24 Jer. xxxi, 22.
25 Votive Mass of Our Lady; Gradual.

losing nothing of His Immensity, so we must allow ourselves to be contained and guided perfectly without reserve, by the humble Mary.

The Inaccessible drew near to us, united Himself closely, perfectly and even personally to our humanity through Mary, losing nothing of His Majesty; so we must draw near to God and unite ourselves perfectly and closely to His Majesty through Mary, without fear of being rejected.

Lastly, He Who Is deigned to come to that which is not, and make that which is not become God or He Who Is; and He did this perfectly by giving and submitting Himself entirely to the youthful Virgin Mary, without ceasing to be in time He Who Is from all eternity. In like manner we, who are nothing, can, through Mary, become like to God by grace and glory, through giving ourselves to her so perfectly and entirely that we are nothing in ourselves but everything in her, without fear of deceiving ourselves.

158. Were a new way made for me to go to Jesus Christ, a way paved with all the merits of the Blessed, adorned with all their heroic virtues, illuminated and beautified by all the radiance and beauty of the angels, were all the angels and saints on that way to lead, defend and sustain those who wished to tread it, truly, truly, I boldly declare, and I speak the truth, that in preference even to such a perfect way I would take the immaculate way of Mary, *Posui immaculatam viam meam,*[26] the way without stain or spot, without sin, actual or original, without shadow or darkness, and if—as is certain—my loving Jesus comes in glory a second time upon earth, there to reign, He will choose no other path for His coming than the divine Mary, through. whom He came the first time so surely and perfectly. The difference between the first and last coming is that the first was secret and hidden, and the second will be

26   Ps. xvii, 33.

glorious, and resplendent; but both of them perfect, for both will be through Mary. Alas! here is a mystery which is not understood: *Hic taceat omnis lingua.*[27]

4. This devotion is a secure way.

159. This devotion to Our Lady is a *secure* way to go to Jesus and to acquire perfection by uniting us with Him: (i) Because the devotion which I teach is not new. It is of such old standing that M. Boudon[28]—who died a short time ago in the odour of sanctity—says in a book which he wrote on this devotion, that the date of its origin cannot be fixed with any precision; it is, however, certain that for more than seven hundred years we find traces of it in the Church.[29]

St Odilon, Abbot of Cluny, who lived about the year 1040, was one of the first to practise it publicly in France, as is narrated in his life.

Cardinal Peter Damien[30] relates that in the year 1016, his brother, Blessed Marino, became the slave of the Blessed Virgin in the presence of his spiritual director in a most edifying manner, for he placed a rope around his neck, scourged himself, and placed on the altar a sum of money as a token of his devotion and consecration to Our Lady. He continued this so faithfully all his life that he merited to be visited and consoled at his death by this loving Mistress, and receive from her lips the promise of paradise in reward for his service.

Caesarius Bollandus mentions a famous knight, Vautier de Birbak, closely related to the Dukes of Louvain, who about the year 1300 consecrated himself to the Blessed Virgin.

27 "Let every tongue be silent here."
28 Doctor of Divinity and Archdeacon at Evreux; author of a work on *The Holy Slavery of the Admirable Mother of God,* and of many other books imbued with an ardent devotion to Our Lady.
29 The pious King Dagobert (seventh century) consecrated himself to Our Lady as her slave. So did Pope John VII (701-707).
30 Made a Doctor of the Church by Leo XII.

This devotion was also practised by many privately, up to the seventeenth century, when it became public.

160. Father Simon de Rojas, of the Order of the Holy Trinity for the Redemption of Captives, court preacher to Philip III, made this devotion popular throughout Spain[31] and Germany[32], and through the intervention of Philip III, obtained from Gregory XV great indulgences for those who practised it.

Father de Los Rios, of the Order of St Augustine, together with his intimate friend, Father De Rojas, devoted himself by word and writing to propagating it throughout Spain and Germany.[33] He composed an imposing volume entitled *Hierarchia Mariana*,[34] wherein with as much piety as erudition, he treats of the antiquity, the excellence and the solidity of this devotion.[35]

The Theatine Fathers, in the seventeenth century, established this devotion in Italy, Sicily and Savoy.

161. Father Stanislaus Phalacius of the Company of Jesus, spread this devotion wonderfully in Poland.[36]

Father de Los Rios, in the book quoted above, names princes, princesses, dukes and cardinals of different kingdoms who embraced this devotion.

Cornelius a Lapide, noted for his piety and his profound learning, was commissioned by several bishops and theologians to examine this devotion, and after mature examination gave it praise worthy of his piety; and several other distinguished persons followed his example.

---

31 In the year 1611.

32 The Emperor Ferdinand II himself made the Consecration in the presence of all his Court, in 1640.

33 He established this devotion in Belgium with Louvain, Malines and Brussels as principal centres.

34 Published in Antwerp in 1641.

35 Approved by the Bishops of Malines, Cambrai and Ghent.

36 Vladislaf IV, King of Poland, was enrolled at Louvain and he asked the Jesuit Fathers to preach this devotion throughout his kingdom.

The Jesuit Fathers, always zealous in the service of Our Blessed Lady, presented, in the name of the Sodalists of Cologne, a little treatise on this devotion[37] to the Duke Ferdinand of Bavaria, the then Archbishop of Cologne, who gave it his approbation and granted permission to print it, exhorting all priests and religious of his diocese to do their utmost to spread this solid devotion.

162. Cardinal de Bérulle, of blessed memory throughout France, was one of the most zealous in spreading this devotion in France, despite the calumny and persecution levelled against him by critics and libertines. They accused him of innovation and superstition. They wrote and published a libel against him, and used, or rather, through their instrumentality the devil used a thousand wiles to hinder him in the spreading of this devotion in France. But this eminent and holy man answered their calumny in patience, and he replied to the objections contained in their libel with a little book in which he refutes them vigorously, pointing out to them that this devotion is founded on the example of Jesus Christ, on the obligations that we have towards Him and on the vows which we made in Holy Baptism. It was particularly with this last reason that he silenced his enemies, showing them that this consecration to the Most Blessed Virgin and, through her hands, to Jesus Christ, is nothing else but a perfect renewal of the vows and promises of Baptism. He makes many beautiful comments on this devotion which can be read in his works.

163. In M. Boudon's book we read of the different Popes who have approved this devotion, the theologians who have examined it, the persecutions it has suffered and overcome, the thousands who embraced it without being condemned by any Pope. Indeed, it could not be condemned without overthrowing the foundations of Christianity.

---

37   Entitled *Mancipium Virginis:* "Slavery of the Blessed Virgin." Cologne 1634.

It is clear, then, that this doctrine is not new and that if it is uncommon the reason is that it is too precious to be appreciated and practised by everyone.[38]

164. (ii) This devotion is a *secure* means of going to Jesus Christ, because it is characteristic of Our Blessed Lady to lead us securely to Jesus Christ, just as it is characteristic of Jesus Christ to lead us to the Eternal Father. Let not spiritual persons erroneously believe that Mary is a hindrance to them in attaining divine union. How could it be possible that she who found grace before God for all in general and everyone in particular could prevent a soul from attaining the great grace of union with Him? How could it be possible that she who is filled to overflowing with graces, who is so united to and transformed into God that it became necessary,[39] for Him to be made flesh in her, should prevent a soul from being perfectly united to Him?

It is quite true that contact with other creatures, although holy, could perhaps at certain times delay divine union; not so with Our Lady, as I have said and shall never weary of repeating. One reason why so few souls come to the fulness of the age of Jesus Christ is that Mary, who is still as much as ever the Mother of the Son and the fruitful Spouse of the Holy Ghost, is not sufficiently formed in their hearts. Whoever desires a ripe and perfectly formed fruit must have the tree that produces it. Whoever desires the Fruit of life, Jesus Christ, must have the tree of life, which is Mary. Whosoever desires to have the Holy Ghost working within him must have His faithful and inseparable Spouse, the divine Mary, through whom He produces and bears fruit, as I have said elsewhere.[40]

---

38 Boudon in his book says that English Catholics were remarkable for the practice of this devotion.

39 Cf. No. 39.

40 Cf. Nos. 20-21.

165. Be persuaded, then, that the more you behold Mary in your prayers, meditations, actions and sufferings, if not with a clear and distinct view, at least with a general and indistinct one, the more perfectly will you find Jesus Christ, who is always, with Mary, great, powerful, operative and incomprehensible, more than in heaven or in any other creature in the universe. Thus, so far from the divine Mary, wholly wrapt in God, being an obstacle to the perfect in attaining their union with God, there has never been till now and there never will be, any creature who will help us more efficaciously in this great work because of the graces she will communicate to us to this effect—for, as a Saint has said, no one can be filled with the thought of God, except by her: *Nemo cogitatione Dei repletur nisi per te*[41] or because of her safeguarding us against the illusions and wiles of the Evil One.

166. Where Mary is, there the Evil One is not; and one of the most infallible signs that we are led by the Spirit of God is our being really devoted to Mary, frequently thinking and speaking of her. This is the opinion of a Saint,[42] who adds that as breathing is a sure sign that the body is not dead, so the frequent thought and loving invocation of Mary is a sure sign that the soul is not dead in sin.

167. Since Mary alone has crushed all heresies, as we are told by the Church guided by the Holy Ghost: *Sola cunctas haereses interemisti in universo mundo,*[43] though critics may protest, a faithful devotee of Mary will never fall into heresy or illusion, at least formally. He may very well fall into material error, taking lies for truth, the evil spirit for the good—though less easily than others —but sooner or later he will recognise it, will not stubbornly believe and maintain what he believed to be the truth.

---

41 St Germanus of Constantinople. *(Sermo 2ª in Dormitione.)*
42 St Germanus of Constantinople. *(Sermo in Encaenia venerandae aedis B.V.)*
43 Office of the Blessed Virgin.

168. Whoever, then, wishes—without fear of those illusions, which are so common with men of prayer—to advance in the way of perfection and surely and perfectly to find Jesus Christ, let him take up *corde magno et animo volenti,* "with a great heart and a willing mind,"[44] this devotion to the Blessed Virgin, which perhaps he had not hitherto known. Let him enter into this excellent way, hitherto unknown to him and which I now show him: *excellentiorem viam vobis demonstro*[45]—"I show you a more excellent way." It is a way opened by Jesus Christ, the Incarnate Wisdom, our only Head; His members cannot be deceived in using it.

It is an *easy* way because of the plenitude of grace and the unction of the Holy Ghost which fill it, in treading it we do not tire or fall back. It is a *short* way which in a short time leads us to Jesus Christ. It is a *perfect* way in which there is neither mud, nor dust, nor the least vileness of sin. Finally it is a *secure* way which directly and safely, without turning to right or left leads us to Jesus and to life eternal.

Let us, then, take this way, travelling along it night and day even to the fulness of the age of Jesus Christ.

ARTICLE VI.

This devotion gives great interior liberty.

169. *Sixth motive.* The practice of this devotion gives great interior liberty—the liberty of the children of God[46]—to those who faithfully practise it. For as, by this devotion, we become slaves of Jesus Christ, consecrating ourselves entirely to Him in this capacity, this good Master rewarding the loving captivity we take upon ourselves, (i) delivers us from all such scruples and servile fear as would narrow, imprison, and

---

44 2 Mach. i, 3.
45 1 Cor. xii, 31.
46 Rom. viii, 21.

perplex our soul; (ii) broadens our heart with holy confidence in God, making us look upon Him as our Father; (iii) breathes into us a tender and filial love.

170. Without stopping to prove these truths by arguments, I shall content myself with quoting an historical fact that I have read in the life of Mother Agnes of Jesus, a Dominican nun of the Convent of Langeac, in Auvergne, who died there in the odour of sanctity of 1634. When she was but seven years old, and suffering from great spiritual trials, she heard a voice telling her that if she wished to be delivered from all her anxieties and protected against all her enemies, she should make herself immediately the slave of Jesus and His Blessed Mother. No sooner had she returned home than she gave herself entirely as a slave to Jesus and His Mother, although up to that time she had known absolutely nothing of this devotion. Finding an iron chain she bound it round her loins and wore it to the day of her death. After this action, all her trials and scruples ceased, and she found great peace and liberty of heart; this led her to teach this devotion to many others, who made great progress in it; among them were M. Olier, the founder of St Sulpice, and a number of priests and ecclesiastics of the same Seminary. One day, the Blessed Virgin appeared to her and placed around her neck a chain of gold, in token of the joy she felt that she had become her Son's slave and her own. St Cecilia, who accompanied Our Lady, said to her: "Happy are the faithful slaves of the Queen of Heaven, because they shall enjoy true liberty": *Tibi servire libertas.*

ARTICLE VII.

By this devotion we greatly benefit our neighbour.

171. *Seventh motive.* Another reason urging us to adopt this devotion is the great benefit which accrues to our neighbour from it. For by this practice we exercise charity towards him in a most eminent manner, for we give him, through the hands of Mary, all our most precious possessions, which are the satisfactory and impetratory value of all our good works without excepting the least good thought or the least little suffering. We consent that any satisfaction we have acquired or will acquire until the day of our death should be used, according to the will of Our Blessed Lady, for the conversion of sinners or the relief of the souls in Purgatory.

Is not this perfect love of our neighbour? Is not this being the true disciple of Jesus Christ, who is known by charity?[47] Is not this the means of converting sinners, without any fear of vain glory; and of delivering souls from Purgatory, by doing scarcely anything more than what we are obliged to do in our state of life?

172. To appreciate the excellence of this motive, we should have to understand how good a thing it is to convert a sinner or to deliver a soul from Purgatory: something infinitely good, greater than the creation of heaven and earth,[48] for we give to a soul the possession of God. If by this devotion we should release but one soul from Purgatory, or convert but one sinner in our whole lifetime, would not this be enough to induce every charitable man to embrace it?

But it must be noted that, passing through the hands of Mary, our good works receive an increase of purity, and in consequence, of merit and satisfactory and impetratory value. This is why they are far more capable of relieving the souls in Purgatory and of converting sinners than if they did not pass through the, virginal and liberal hands of Mary. The little that we give through Mary, stripped as it is of self-will and flowing from disinterested charity, becomes, in truth, most powerful

---

47   John xiii, 35.
48   St Augustine *(Tract. 72 in Joan)*.

to calm the wrath of God and draw down His mercy. It may well be that at the hour of death a person who has been faithful to this practice will find that he has thus delivered many souls from Purgatory and converted many sinners, although he has performed only the ordinary actions of his state in life. What joy at his judgment! What glory throughout eternity!

ARTICLE VIII.

This devotion is an admirable means of perseverance.

173. *Eighth motive.* Finally, what draws us in a sense more powerfully towards this devotion to the Most Blessed Virgin is that it is a wondrous means of persevering in virtue and remaining faithful. For why is it that the majority of the conversions of sinners are not lasting? Why is it that we relapse so easily into sin? Why is it that the greater part of the faithful, instead of advancing from virtue to virtue and acquiring new graces, often lose the little grace and virtue they possess? This evil springs, as I have already shown,[49] from the fact that man, being so corrupt, so weak and so fickle trusts in himself, relies on his own strength and believes himself capable of safeguarding the treasure of his graces, of his virtues and his merits.

By this devotion, we confide to Mary, the faithful Virgin, all we possess; we choose her as the universal guardian of all our possessions in the order of nature and of grace. It is in her fidelity that we trust, on her strength that we rely, on her mercy and charity that we base ourselves, so that she may guard and increase our virtues and merits despite the devil, the world and the flesh, who strive to rob us of them. Like a child to its mother, a faithful servant to his mistress, we say to her: *Depositum custodi;*[50] My gentle Mother and Mistress, I

---

49 Cf. Nos. 87-89.
50 Tim. vi, 20.

acknowledge that till this moment I have received from God, through thine intercession, more graces than I have merited; unhappy experience teaches me that I carry this treasure in a most fragile vessel and that I am too weak and wretched to guard it by myself: *Adolescentulus sum ego et contemptus.*[51] I beseech thee receive in trust all that I possess and by thy fidelity and power keep it for me. If thou dost watch over me, I shall lose nothing; if thou dost uphold me, I shall not fall; if thou dost protect me, I am shielded from all my enemies.

174. This is what St Bernard says in explicit terms, to encourage us to adopt this practice: "When Mary upholds you, you will not fall; when she protects you, you need not fear; when she leads you, you will not weary; when she is favourable to you, you will reach the harbour of salvation." *Ipsa tenente, non corruis; ipsa protegente, non metuis; ipsa duce, non fatigaris; ipsa propitia, pervenis* (Serm. super *Missus est*). St Bonaventure seems to say the same thing in more explicit terms: "The Blessed Virgin," he says, "not only is retained in the plenitude of the Saints, but she also keeps the saints in their plenitude, lest it should diminish. She keeps their virtues, lest they be scattered, their merits lest they be wasted and their graces lest they be lost; she keeps the devil from doing them harm; she keeps her divine Son from punishing them, when they sin": *Virgo non solum in plenitudine Sanctorum detinetur, sed etiam in plenitudine sanctos detinet, ne plenitudo minuatur: detinet virtutes ne fugiant; detinet merita ne pereant; detinet gratias ne effluant; detinet daemones ne noceant; detinet Filium ne peccatores percutiat* (St Bonav., In Speculo B.V.).

175. The Most Blessed Virgin is that faithful virgin who by her fidelity to God makes good the losses caused by the faithlessness of disloyal Eve; and for those who attach themselves to her she obtains fidelity to God and perseverance.

---

51 Ps. cxviii, 141.

That is why a Saint compares her to a firm anchor, which holds them fast and saves them from shipwreck in the raging sea of the world, where so many people perish for not being attached to this firm anchor. "We bind souls," says he, "to thy hope, as to a firm anchor."—*Animas ad spem tuam sicut ad firmam anchoram alligamus.*[52] It was to her that the saints who reached salvation most firmly bound themselves and others in order to persevere in virtue. Happy then, a thousand times happy, are the Christians who attach themselves to her faithfully and entirely as to a firm anchor! The violence of the storms of this world will not make them founder, nor tear from them their heavenly treasures. Happy those who enter into her as into the Ark of Noah! The waters of the deluge of sin which drown so many will not harm them, because, says Mary with the Divine Wisdom:—*Qui operantur in me non peccabunt:*[53] Those who work in me for their salvation shall not sin. Happy are the unfaithful children of unhappy Eve who attach themselves to the faithful Virgin and Mother, who remains always faithful and never belies herself: *Fidelis permanet, seipsam negate non potest,*[54] and who always loves those who love her: *Ego diligentes me diligo,*[55] not only with an affective love but with an active and efficacious love, keeping them, by a great abundance of grace, from failing in the practice of virtue or falling by the wayside by losing her Son's grace.

176. Out of pure charity, this good Mother always receives whatever is entrusted to her; and once she has received something in deposit, she is obliged in justice, by virtue of the contract of trusteeship, to keep it safely for us; just as some one to whom I might entrust a thousand pounds would be obliged

---

52 St John Damascene. *(Sermo in Dormitione B.M.V.)*
53 Eccli. xxiv, 30.
54 2 Tim. ii, 13.
55 Prov. viii, 17.

to keep them safely for me, so that if they were lost through his negligence he would be responsible for them in justice. But no, never will anything we entrust to the faithful Mary be lost through negligence. Heaven and earth would pass away sooner than Mary could be negligent and unfaithful to those who trust in her.

177. Poor children of Mary, your weakness is extreme, your fickleness is great, your human nature thoroughly corrupt. You are drawn, I admit, from the same corrupt mass as the children of Adam and Eve; yet be not discouraged because of that, but be consoled and rejoice; learn the secret which I am teaching you, a secret unknown to almost all Christians, even the most devout.

Do not leave your gold and silver in your own coffers, already broken into by the Evil Spirit who robbed you, and which are too small, too weak and too old to contain so great and precious a treasure. Do not put pure and limpid spring water in vessels fouled and infected by sin; even if sin is no longer there, the stench remains, and the water would be tainted by it. Do not put your exquisite wines in old casks which have been used for bad wine, they would be spoiled and run the danger of being spilled.

178. Predestined souls, although you already understand me I shall speak still more clearly. Do not trust the gold of your charity, the silver of your purity, the waters of heavenly grace, or the wines of your merits and virtues to a torn sack, a broken, old coffer, or a tainted and corrupt cask such as you are. Otherwise you will be stripped by robbers, the devils, who, night and day, seek and spy out for a favourable opportunity to do so;[56] otherwise you will taint with the stench of self-love, self-reliance, and self-confidence all the most pure gifts of God.

---

56 St Gregory the Great.

Pour into the bosom and heart of Mary all your treasures, all your graces and virtues. She is the spiritual vessel, the vessel of honour, the singular vessel of devotion: *Vas spirituale, vas honorabile, vas insigne devotionis.* Ever since God personally hid Himself away, together with all His perfections, in this vessel, it has become completely spiritual, and the spiritual abode of all most spiritual souls; it has become honourable and the throne of honour of the greatest princes of eternity; it has become singular in devotion and the dwelling place of the most illustrious in gentleness, in grace and in virtue. Finally, it has become rich as a house of gold, strong as a tower of David, pure as a tower of ivory.

179. Oh! how happy is the man who has given everything to Mary, who, in everything and for everything trusts to Mary; and is absorbed in her! He is all Mary's and Mary is all his. He can say confidently with David: *Haec facta est mihi.*[57]—"Mary is made for me"; or with the beloved disciple: *Accepi eam in mea.*[58]—"I have taken her for my all"; or with Jesus Christ: *Omnia mea tua sunt, et omnia tua mea sunt.* "All that I have is thine, and all that thou hast is mine."

180. If any critic, reading this, should imagine that I am exaggerating and speaking from excessive devotion, he does not, alas, understand me either because he is a carnal man who does not savour the things of the spirit,[59] or because, being of the world, he cannot receive the Holy Ghost, or because being proud and critical he despises and condemns all that he does not understand. But souls which are born not of blood, nor of flesh, nor of the will, of man, but of God and of Mary understand and appreciate what I say, and it is for them I write.

---

57 Ps. cxviii, 56.
58 John xvii, 10.
59 John i, 13.

181. Nevertheless, after this digression, I say both to the former as well as to the latter, that the divine Mary, being the most trustworthy and liberal of all mere creatures, never lets herself be outdone in love and generosity; and as a holy man has said, for a penny she gives a pound,[60] that is to say, for the little that is given to her, she gives much of what she has received from God. Consequently, if a soul gives himself to her without reserve, she gives herself to that soul, also without reserve, provided he place unpresuming confidence in her, striving, for his part, to acquire virtue and bridle his passions.

182. So let faithful servants of the Blessed Virgin say boldly with St John Damascene: "With confidence in thee, O Mother of God, I shall be saved; with thy protection I shall fear nothing; with thy help, I shall fight and disperse all my enemies; for devotion to thee is a weapon of salvation which God gives to those whom He wishes to save." *Spent tuam habens, O Deipara, servabor; defensionem tuam possidens, non tiniebo; persequar inimicos meos et in fugam vertam, habens protectionem tuam, et auxilium tuum; nam tibi devotum esse est arma quaedam salutis quae Deus his dat quos vult salvos fieri.* (Joan. Damas. Serm. de Annun.)

---

60 The French text says "Un œuf pour un bœuf"—an *egg* for an ox.

CHAPTER SIX.

BIBLICAL FIGURE OF THIS PERFECT DEVOTION: REBECCA AND JACOB.

183. The Holy Ghost gives us in the Scriptures[1] a wonderful figure of all the truths that I have written down concerning Our Blessed Lady, her children and servants. It is the story of Jacob, who received the blessing of his father, Isaac, through the care and ingenuity of Rebecca, his mother.

Here is the story as the Holy Ghost relates it. I shall later add the explanation.

ARTICLE I.

Rebecca and Jacob.

1. Story of Jacob.

184. When Esau sold his birthright to Jacob, Rebecca, their mother, who tenderly loved Jacob, obtained for him the advantage of this birthright several years later by means of an act of ingenuity which was at once most holy and full of mystery. For Isaac, realising his old age and wishing to bless his children before death, called Esau whom he loved and commanded him to go hunting to obtain food, that he might afterwards bless him. Rebecca immediately warned Jacob of what was happening and ordered him to take two kids from the flock. When he had given them to his mother, she prepared for Isaac a dish which she knew he liked, dressed Jacob in the garments of Esau—which were in her charge—and covered his hands and neck with the kid-skins, so that the father, who was blind, though hearing the voice of Jacob, might be-

---

1 Gen. xxvii.

lieve from the skin on his hands that he was his brother Esau. And indeed, surprised at the voice, which he thought was that of Jacob, Isaac bade him approach; then, having touched the hairy skins with which Jacob's hands were covered, he said that the voice indeed was the voice of Jacob, but the hands were the hands of Esau. Then, when he had eaten and, in kissing Jacob, had smelt the perfume of his garments he blessed him and called down upon him the dew of heaven and the fatness of the earth. He made him master of his brothers and finished the blessing with these words: "Cursed be he that curseth thee and let him that blesseth thee be filled with blessings."

Isaac had scarce finished these words when Esau entered carrying the dish of what he had caught in hunting, that his father might afterwards bless him. The holy patriarch was struck with unbelievable astonishment when he realised what had happened, but, far from retracting what he had done, he confirmed it, seeing all too plainly the finger of God in these happenings. Then, as the Scripture relates, Esau broke into furious cries, and loudly accusing his brother of treachery, asked his father if he had but one blessing. And in this, as the holy Fathers point out, he was at one with those who, seeking to ally God with the world, would fain enjoy the consolations of both earth and heaven. Touched by the cries of Esau, Isaac finally blessed him, but with a blessing of the earth, subjecting him to his brother. From this Esau conceived so venomous a hatred of Jacob that he only awaited the death of his father to kill him. Nor could Jacob have escaped death if his loving mother Rebecca had not preserved him from it by her efforts and the good advice which she gave him and which he followed.

2. Interpretation of the story of Jacob.

185. Before an explanation of this beautiful story, it must be observed that, according to all the Holy Fathers and interpreters of Scripture, Jacob is the figure of Jesus Christ and the predestinate, and Esau the figure of the reprobate; we have but to examine the actions and the conduct of one and the other to pronounce judgment.

(i) Esau, figure of the Reprobate.

1. Esau, the elder, was strong and robust of body, adroit and skilful with the bow, and very successful in taking game.

2. He seldom stayed at home, and relying on his strength and skill, worked only out of doors.

3. He was not very concerned with pleasing his mother, Rebecca, and did nothing for that end.

4. So greedy was he, so fond of eating, that he sold his birthright for a mess of pottage.

5. He was, like Cain, extremely jealous of his brother Jacob, and persecuted him beyond measure.

186. Such is the daily conduct of the reprobate.

1. They trust in their own strength and skill in temporal affairs; they are very proficient, very clever and very enlightened in the things of this world, but very dull and very ignorant in the things of heaven; *In terrenis fortes, in coelestibus debiles.* For this reason:

187. 2. They spend but little time at home, in their own house, that is in their interior which is the internal and essential abode which God has given to every man, there to dwell after His own example: for God remains always within Himself. The reprobate do not like a retired and spiritual life of interior devotion, and they look on those who live interiorly, secluded from the world, working more within than without, as narrow-minded, sanctimonious and uncivilised creatures.

188. 3. The reprobate cares little for devotion to Mary, the Mother of the predestinate. It is true that they have no formal hatred for her; they sometimes praise her, they say that they love her, they even practise some devotion in her honour; but apart from that they cannot bear that she should be tenderly loved, for they have none of the tenderness of Jacob. They find fault with the practices of devotion which her faithful children and servants use to gain her affection, for they hold that such devotion is in no way necessary to salvation, and that it is enough not explicitly to hate her, or openly despise devotion to her. They think they gain the favour of the Blessed Virgin, they think they serve her by reciting and mumbling some prayers in her honour, without tenderness towards her or amendment in themselves.

189. 4. The reprobate sell their birthright, that is to say, the joys of paradise, for a mess of pottage; that is to say, for the joys of earth. They laugh, they drink, they eat, they amuse themselves, they play, they dance, etc., and take no more trouble than Esau to become worthy of the blessing of the Heavenly Father. In a word, they think only of the earth; they love only the earth; they speak and act only for the earth and its pleasures; and for one brief moment of pleasure, for a puff of honour, for a piece of hard earth, be it yellow or white, they sell their baptismal grace, their robe of innocence, their heavenly inheritance.

190. 5. Finally, the reprobate continually hate and persecute the predestinate, openly or in secret; the predestinate are a burden to them, they despise, them, criticize them, ridicule them, insult them, rob them, deceive them, impoverish them; hunt them down and lay them in the dust; whilst they themselves are making their fortune, enjoying themselves, holding good positions, enriching themselves, rising to power and living in comfort.

(ii) Jacob, figure of the Predestinate.

191. 1. Jacob, the younger son, was of a weak constitution, gentle and peaceful, and usually stayed at home, in order to win the affection of his mother, Rebecca, whom he dearly loved. If he did go out it was through no personal desire, nor from any confidence in his own ability, but simply to obey his mother.

192. 2. He loved and honoured his mother, and for that reason remained at home, near her. He was never more content than when he saw her. Everything that might displease her he carefully avoided, and did everything he thought might please her. All this increased Rebecca's love for him.

193. 3. In all things he was submissive to his beloved mother. He obeyed her entirely in everything, promptly without delay, and lovingly without ever a complaint. At the least manifestation of her will the little Jacob would run and work. He believed everything she told him, without any argument, as for example, when she told him to go and fetch two kids and bring them to her that she might prepare a dish for his father Isaac. Jacob did not reply that one would be quite enough for one man to eat; without argument, he did as she bade him.

194. 4. He had the utmost confidence in his beloved mother. As he did not rely on his own ability, he depended solely upon the care and protection of his mother. He appealed to her in all his needs and consulted her in all his doubts. For example, when he asked her whether his father, instead of blessing him, would curse him, he believed her and trusted her when she said she would take the curse upon herself.

195. 5. Finally, he imitated, as far as he could, the virtues he beheld in his mother. It would seem, indeed, that one of his reasons for remaining so much at home was the desire to imitate his mother who was so virtuous, and to avoid evil company which corrupts morals. In this way, he made himself worthy to receive the twofold blessing of his beloved father.

196. Such is also the daily conduct of the predestinate.

1. They remain at home with their mother. That is to say, they love retirement and the interior life; they are assiduous

in prayer, but after the example and in the company of their Mother, the Blessed Virgin, whose glory is wholly within, and who, during her lifetime, loved retirement and prayer so dearly. True, they are sometimes to be seen in the outer world, but it is in obedience to the will of God and that of their beloved Mother, in the fulfilment of their duty of state. However great their exterior work may appear, they themselves attach far more importance to what they do inwardly, in their interior life, in company with the Blessed Virgin, for there they work out the great task of perfection in comparison with which all other labours are mere child's play. It is on this account that, while sometimes their brothers and sisters busy themselves about exterior works with much energy, industry and success, winning the praise and approbation of the world, they, on the contrary, know by the light of the Holy Ghost that it is far more glorious, better and more delightful to remain hidden in retirement with Jesus Christ their Model, in an entire subjection to their Mother, than it is to perform, by oneself, wonders of nature and of grace in the world, like so many Esaus and reprobates. *Gloria et divitiae in domo ejus,*[2] The glory of God and the wealth of men are to be found in the house of Mary.

O Lord Jesus, how lovely are Thy tabernacles! The sparrow has found a house wherein to dwell; and the turtle-dove a nest for her little ones. Oh, how happy is the man who dwells in the house of Mary, where Thou wert the first to take up Thy abode. In this house of the predestinate he receives help from Thee alone and sets up in his heart the steps and degrees of all virtues whereby to climb to perfection in this vale of tears. *Quam dilecta tabernacula,* etc.[3]

197. 2. The predestinate tenderly love and truly honour Our Blessed Lady as their good Mother and Mistress. They

---

2 Ps. cxi, 3.
3 Ps. lxxxiii, 1.

love her not in word only, but in truth; they honour her not merely externally, but from the bottom of their hearts. Like Jacob, they shun all that could displease her and fervently practise whatever they think will find them favour with her. They bring to her and give her, not two kids as Jacob did to Rebecca, but their body and soul and everything depending thereon, as symbolised by the two kids of Jacob; in order: (i) that she may receive them as her own; (ii) that she may kill them and make them die to sin and self, flaying them, stripping them of their own skin, which is their self-love, and thus making them pleasing to Jesus her Son, who wishes to have as friends and disciples only those who are dead to themselves; (iii) that she may dress them to the taste of their Heavenly Father, and for His greater glory, which she knows better than any other creature; and (iv) that by her care and intercession this body and soul, thoroughly cleansed from every stain, thoroughly dead, thoroughly stripped and well prepared, may be a choice dish pleasing to the taste of the heavenly Father and meriting His blessing. Is not this the conduct of the predestinate who, to prove to Jesus and Mary their effective and courageous love, will relish and practise the perfect consecration to Jesus through the hands of Mary, which we teach them?

The reprobate say easily that they love Jesus, that they love and honour Mary, but they do not love them with their substance,[4] and, unlike the predestinate, do not love them enough to sacrifice to them their body with its senses and their soul with its passions.

198. 3. The predestinate are subject and obedient to Our Blessed Lady, as to their beloved Mother, after the example of Jesus Christ, who, of the three and thirty years He lived on earth, devoted thirty to glorifying God His Father by perfect and entire submission to His holy Mother. They obey her,

---

4 Prov. iii, 9.

following her advice to the letter, just as the youthful Jacob followed that of Rebecca, who said to him: *Acquiesce consiliis meis.*[5] "My son, follow my counsels"; or like the waiters at the marriage feast of Cana to whom Our Lady said: *Quodcumque dixerit vobis facite*[6]—"Whatever my Son shall say to you, do ye." Through obedience to his mother, Jacob received the blessing as it were by a miracle, although naturally he should not have had it. In reward for following the advice of Our Blessed Lady, the waiters of the Wedding Feast of Cana were honoured with the first of Christ's miracles, when at the prayer of this Blessed Mother, He changed the water into wine. Even so, till the end of time, all who receive the blessing of the Heavenly Father and are honoured with the wonders of God, will receive these graces only in consequence of their perfect obedience to Mary. On the contrary, the Esaus lose their blessing because of lack of submission to the Blessed Virgin.

199. 4. They have great confidence in the goodness and power of the Most Blessed Virgin, their beloved Mother; incessantly they implore her help, they look on her as their Polar Star to guide them to safe haven; with great openness of heart they disclose to her their troubles and their needs; they cling to her breasts of mercy and gentleness to obtain pardon for sin by her intercession and to taste her maternal sweetness in their troubles and anxieties. In a wondrous manner, they cast themselves into, hide and lose themselves in her loving and virginal bosom, there to be enkindled with the fire of pure love, to be cleansed from every least stain, and to find perfectly Jesus, who dwells there as on His most glorious throne. Oh! what happiness! "Think not," says the Abbot Guerric, "that there is more joy in dwelling in Abraham's bosom than in Mary's, seeing that Our Lord has placed His throne in her." —*Ne cre-*

---

5   Gen. xxvii, 8.
6   John ii, 5.

dideris majoris esse felicitatis habitate in sinu Abrahae quam in sinu Mariae, cum in eo Dominus posuerit thronum suum.[7]

The reprobate, on the contrary, relying entirely on themselves, eating with the Prodigal Son, the husks of the swine; feeding on earth like toads and, with the worldly, loving only the visible and exterior things, have no relish for the sweetness of Mary's bosom. They do not feel that reliance and confidence which the predestinate feel for the Blessed Virgin, their beloved Mother. They miserably love to hunger after the things that are without, as St Gregory says,[8] for they do not wish to taste the sweetness already prepared within them and in Jesus and Mary.

200. 5. Finally, the predestinate keep the ways of the Blessed Virgin, their loving Mother, that is, they imitate her, and thus they are truly happy and devout, and bear the infallible sign of their predestination, as this loving Mother says of them: *Beati qui custodiunt vias meas,*[9] which means, blessed are they who practise my virtues, and who, by the help of God's grace, walk in the footsteps of my life. During their life they are happy in this world, by reason of the abundance of grace and sweetness which I impart to them of my fullness, and more abundantly than to others, who do not imitate me so closely; they are happy at death, which for them is sweet and peaceful and at which I am usually present to lead them myself to the joys of eternity, for never has there been lost one of my good servants, who during life imitated my virtues.

The reprobate, on the contrary, are unhappy during their life, at their death and throughout eternity, because they do not imitate the virtues of the Most Blessed Virgin, being satisfied with sometimes joining her Confraternities, reciting

---

7 *Sermo in Assumptione*, No. 4.
8 *Amamus foris miseri famem nostram* (Homil. 36 in Evang.).
9 Prov. viii, 32.

some prayers in her honour or showing some other exterior devotion.

O Blessed Virgin, my beloved Mother, how happy are they, I repeat it in the transports of my heart, how happy are they who, unseduced by false devotion towards thee, faithfully keep thy ways, thy counsels and thy commands. But how unhappy and accursed are they who, abusing devotion towards thee, do not keep the commandments of thy Son: *Maledicti omnes qui declinant a mandatis tuis.*[10]

ARTICLE II.

The Blessed Virgin and her slaves of love.

201. And now, here are the loving services that the Blessed Virgin, best of all mothers, renders to those faithful servants who have given themselves to her, in the manner I have described and according to the figure of Jacob.

I. She loves them.

Ego diligentes me diligo[11]—"I love those who love me." She loves them: (i) because she is their true Mother: now a mother always loves her child, the fruit of her womb; (ii) she loves them out of gratitude because they have for her, their beloved Mother, an effective love; (iii) she loves them because, as they are predestinate, God loves them: *Jacob dilexi. Esau autem odio habui;*[12] (iv) she loves them because they have consecrated themselves entirely to her, and are her portion and her inheritance: *In Israel haereditare.*[13]

202. She loves them tenderly, more tenderly, than all the mothers in the world together. Put, if possible, in the heart

---

10 Ps. cxviii, 21. "Cursed are those who fall away from thy commandments."
11 Prov. viii, 17.
12 Rom. ix, 13. "Jacob I have loved, but Esau I have hated."
13 Eccli. xxiv, 13.

of one mother for an only child the natural love of all the mothers in the world for their children; certainly that mother's love would be immense, yet it is true that Mary loves her children even more tenderly than that mother would love her child.

She loves them not only affectionately but also effectively. Her love for them is active and effective as was Rebecca's love for Jacob, even more so. And here is what this loving Mother, of whom Rebecca was but a figure, does for her children to gain them the blessing of their Heavenly Father.

203. (i) Like Rebecca, she watches for favourable opportunities to do them good, to ennoble and enrich them. As she clearly sees in God all that is good and all that is evil, every good and evil fortune, every blessing and malediction of God, she forestalls events, so as to safeguard her servants from many evils and to impart to them many blessings; so that if there is some good fortune to be made in God by the faithful discharge of some high task, it is certain that Mary will obtain such fortune for one of her beloved children and servants, and will give him the grace to carry it through faithfully. *Ipsa procurat negotia nostra,*[14] says a Saint.

204. (ii) She gives them good counsel, as Rebecca did to Jacob: *Fili mi acquiesce consiliis meis*—"My son, follow my counsels."[15] Among other things, she advises them to bring her the two kids, that is, their body and their soul, and to consecrate them to her, that she may prepare them as a dish pleasing to God; and to observe whatever Jesus Christ, her Son, has taught by word and example. If she does not give these counsels in person, it will be through the ministry of angels whose greatest honour and pleasure it is to come on earth at her command to succour her faithful servants.

---

14 "She manages herself our affairs."
15 Gen. xxvii, 8.

205. (iii) And what does this good Mother do when we have brought and consecrated to her our soul and body with all that depends on them, without exception? She does what Rebecca did in former days to the two kids brought to her by Jacob. (1) She kills them, i.e., she causes them to die to the life of the old Adam; (2) she flays and strips them of their natural skin, i.e., of their natural inclinations, their self-love, self-will and all attachment to creatures; (3) she purifies them from their stains, impurities and sins; (4) she prepares them to the taste of God and to His greater glory. As she alone knows perfectly what is the taste and greater glory of the Most High, she alone, without fear of mistake, can prepare and dress our body and soul to that infinitely exalted taste and that infinitely hidden glory.

206. (iv) Having received the perfect offering we have made of ourselves, our merits and satisfactions, through the devotion of which I have spoken, and having stripped us of our old garments, this good Mother cleanses us and renders us worthy to appear before our Heavenly Father. (1) She clothes us in the clean, new, precious and perfumed garments of Esau the first-born—namely, of Jesus Christ, her Son—which she keeps in her house, that is, which come under her power, for she *is* the treasurer and universal dispenser of the merits and virtues of Jesus Christ, her Son; she gives and communicates them to whom she wills, when she wills, as she wills and in the proportion she wills, as we have seen above.[16] (2) She covers the neck and hands of her servants with the skins of the kids she has killed and flayed, that is to say, she adorns them with the merits and value of their own actions. She kills and deadens in truth all that is impure and imperfect in them; but she does not lose and scatter the good that grace has worked in them; she preserves and augments it to adorn and strengthen

16 Cf. Nos. 25 and 141.

their neck and hands, that is to say, she strengthens them to carry the yoke of their Lord (a yoke is worn upon the neck) and to work wonders for the glory of God and the salvation of their poor brethren. (3) She imparts new perfume and new gracefulness to those garments and adornments by adding to them the garments of her own merits and virtues; these she bequeathed to them at her death, as relates a holy nun of the last century, who died in the odour of sanctity and learnt this by revelation. Thus all her domestics, i.e., all her servants and slaves, are clothed with double garments, those of her Son and her own; *Omnes domestici ejus vestiti sunt duplicibus;*[17] for this reason they have nothing to fear from the cold of Jesus Christ, white as snow, cold that the reprobate, naked and stripped as they are of the merits of Jesus Christ and the Blessed Virgin, will be unable to bear.

207. (v) Finally Mary obtains for them the blessing of the Heavenly Father, although they, being the youngest born and adopted children, should not normally have it. Clad in garments at once quite new, very precious and of very delightful odour, their bodies and souls well prepared and dressed, they confidently approach the couch of their Heavenly Father. He hears their voice and knows it to be the voice of a sinner; He touches their hands covered with skins; He smells the good odour of their garments; with joy He partakes of that which Mary their Mother has prepared for Him and recognising in them the merits and good odour of His Son and His Blessed Mother, (1) He gives them the double blessing, the blessing of the dew of Heaven: *De rore coeli,*[18] namely divine grace which is the seed of glory: *Benedixit nos in omni benedictione spirituali in Christo Jesu;*[19] and the blessing of the fatness of the earth:

---

17 Prov. xxxi, 21.
18 Gen. xxii, 28.
19 Eph. i, 3. "God hath blessed us with every spiritual blessing in Christ Jesus."

De pinguedine terrae,[20] that is to say, this good Father gives them their daily bread and a sufficient abundance of the goods of this earth. (2) He makes them masters of their brethren, the reprobate; not that this supremacy always appears in this ephemeral world[21] where the reprobate often hold dominion. *Peccatores effabuntur et gloriabuntur.*[22] *Vidi impium superexaltatum et elevatum;*[23] but it is true supremacy and will appear clearly in the next world for all eternity, where the just, as the Holy Ghost tells us, shall reign over the nations and rule them: *Dominabuntur populis.*[24] (3) The Divine Majesty, not content with blessing them in their persons and their possessions, blesses also those who bless them, and curses those who curse and persecute them.

II. She provides for them.

208. The second charitable service which Our Lady renders her faithful servants is that she provides them with everything for body and soul. She gives them twofold garments as we have just seen. She nourishes them with the most delicious meats from the banquet of God: she gives them to eat the Bread of Life which she has formed: *A generationibus meis implemini.*[25] My dear children, she says to them, in the words of the Book of Wisdom, be filled with my generation, that is to say, with Jesus, the Fruit of Life, whom I have brought into the world for you.—*Venite, comedite partem meum et bibite vinum quod miscui vobis;*[26] *Comedite et bibite, et inebriamini, carissimi.*[27]

---

20 Gen. xxvii, 28.
21 1 Cor. vii, 31.
22 Ps. xciii, 3 and 4.
23 Ps. xxxvi, 35. "I have seen the wicked highly exalted and lifted up like the Cedars of Lebanon."
24 Wisdom iii, 8.
25 Eccli. xxiv, 26.
26 Prov. ix, 5.
27 Cant, v, 1.

Come, she repeats, in another passage, eat my bread, which is Jesus, and drink the wine of His love, that I have mixed for you with the milk of my breasts. As Mary is the Treasurer and Dispenser of the gifts and graces of the Most High, she puts aside a goodly portion, indeed the best portion, to nourish and sustain her children and her servants. They are fattened on the Living Bread; they are inebriated with the wine that brings forth virgins.[28] They are carried at her breast: *Ad ubera portabimini.*[29] With such ease do they carry the yoke of Christ that they scarcely feel its weight because of the oil of devotion in which she has softened it: *Jugum eorum computrescet a facie olei.*[30]

III. She leads them.

209. The third service which Our Lady renders her faithful servants is to lead and direct them according to the will of her Son. Rebecca led her little Jacob and gave him good advice from time to time, either to obtain for him the blessing of his father, or to save him from the hatred and persecution of his brother, Esau. Mary, who is the Star of the Sea, leads all her faithful servants to safe haven; she shows them the paths of eternal life; she prevents them from taking dangerous steps; she leads them by the hand along the paths of justice; she upholds them when they are about to fall; she raises them when they have fallen; she chides them like a loving mother when they fail; and sometimes she even lovingly chastises them. Can a child that is obedient to Mary, his foster-mother and enlightened guide, go astray in the paths of eternity? *Ipsam sequens non devias:* Following her, you will not stray, says St Bernard. Do not fear that a true child of Mary can be seduced by the

---

28 Zach. ix, 17.
29 Is. lxvi, 12.
30 Is. x, 27.

devil and fall into formal heresy. Where Mary guides, the evil spirit with his illusions, or the heretics with their subtleties are not to be found: *Ipsa tenente non corruis.*[31]

IV. She defends and protects them.

210. The fourth loving service which Our Lady renders her children and faithful servants is to defend and protect them from their enemies. By her care and efforts Rebecca delivered Jacob from all dangers that beset him and particularly from dying at the hands of his brother Esau, as he apparently would have done, because Esau hated and envied him just as Cain hated his brother Abel. Mary, the beloved Mother of the predestinate hides them under her protecting wing as a hen does her chicks. She speaks, she lowers herself to them, she condescends to all their weaknesses. To guard them from the hawk and the vulture she hovers over them, and accompanies them as an army in battle array: *Ut castrorum acies ordinata.*[32] Need anyone surrounded by a well-ordered army of one hundred thousand men fear his enemies? The faithful servant of Mary, surrounded as he is by her protection and imperial power need fear still less. This good Mother, this mighty Princess of Heaven would sooner despatch millions of angels to help one of her servants, than that it should ever be said that a faithful servant of Mary trusted in her and yet succumbed to the malice, the number and strength of his enemies.

V. She intercedes for them.

211. Lastly, the fifth and greatest service which this loving Mother renders her faithful devotees, is to intercede for them with her Son, to appease Him with her prayers, to unite them to Him most intimately and to preserve that union.

---

31   St Bernard. Cf. No. 174.
32   Cant, vi, 3.

Rebecca bade Jacob approach the bed of his father, and the patriarch touched him, embraced him, and even joyfully kissed him, being content and replete with the well-prepared dishes which Jacob had brought him. Then having inhaled with great joy the exquisite perfume of his garments he cried: *Ecce odor filii mei sicut odor agri pleni, cui benedixit Dominus.* "Behold the odour of my son is as the odour of a plentiful field, which the Lord hath blest."[33] This plentiful field, the fragrance of which so charmed the heart of the father, is no other than the fragrance of the merits and virtues of Mary, who is the plentiful field of grace, in which God the Father has sown the grain of wheat of the elect, His only Son.

Oh, how welcome to Jesus Christ, the Father of the world to come[34], is a child perfumed with the fragrance of Mary! Oh, how promptly and how perfectly is such a child united to Him! But this we have already shown at length.

212. Furthermore, when Mary has heaped her favours upon her children and faithful servants, when she has obtained for them the blessing of the Heavenly Father and union with Jesus Christ, she keeps them in Jesus Christ and keeps Jesus Christ in them. She guards them, watches over them day and night, lest they lose the grace of God and fall into the snares of their enemies: *In plenitudine sanctos detinet*—"She keeps the saints in their fulness,"[35] and makes them persevere, as we have said, to the end.

Such is the interpretation of this great and ancient figure of predestination and reprobation, so unknown and so full of mysteries.

---

33 Gen. xxvii, 27.
34 Is. ix, 6.
35 St Bonaventure. Cf. No. 174.

CHAPTER SEVEN.

THE WONDROUS EFFECTS WHICH THIS DEVOTION PRODUCES IN A SOUL THAT IS FAITHFUL TO IT.

213. My dear brother, be sure that if you remain faithful to the interior and exterior practices of this devotion which I will point out,[1] the following effects will be produced in your soul:

ARTICLE I.

First Effect.—Knowledge and contempt of self.

(i) In the light which the Holy Ghost will give you through Mary, His faithful Spouse, you will know the evil residue that is in you, your incapability of any good which does not flow from God as author of nature or of grace, and in consequence of this knowledge, you will despise yourself and think of yourself with horror. You will consider yourself as a snail that spoils everything with its slime; or as a toad, that poisons everything with its venom, or as a crafty serpent, seeking only to deceive. Finally, the humble Mary will share with you her humility with the result that whilst despising yourself and loving to be despised, you will despise no one.

ARTICLE II.

Second Effect.—Participation in Mary's Faith.

214. (ii) The Blessed Virgin will share with you that faith which, when she was on earth, was greater than that of all the Patriarchs, Prophets, Apostles and Saints. Now that she reigns

---

1 Cf. Chapter viii.

in Heaven she no longer has this faith, seeing, as she does, all things clearly in God, by the light of glory. However, it has been pleasing to the Most High that she should not lose it by entering Heaven, but that she should keep it, in order to preserve it in the Church Militant for her faithful servants.[2] Therefore the more you gain the benevolence of this august Princess and faithful Virgin, the more will pure faith be evident in your conduct; a pure faith that will make you care little for sensible and extraordinary feelings; a lively faith animated by charity, enabling you to perform your actions only from the motive of pure love; a faith firm and unshakable as a rock by which you will stand firm and steadfast in the midst of storms and tempests; an active and piercing faith, which, like some mysterious master-key, will give you admittance to the mysteries of Jesus Christ, the last end of man, and to the heart of God Himself; a courageous faith, by which you will unhesitatingly undertake and carry through great things for God and the salvation of souls. Lastly, a faith which will be your blazing torch, your divine life, your hidden treasure of divine Wisdom, and the all-powerful weapon you will use to enlighten those who walk in darkness and the shadow of death, to inflame those who are lukewarm and need the burning gold of charity, to give life to those who are dead in sin, to move and convert by gentle and convincing word hearts of marble and cedars of Lebanon;[3] and lastly to resist the devil and all enemies of salvation.

---

2 This passage has been much discussed and criticised. The Auditors, however, at De Montfort's Beatification, raised no objection to it. Mary, in heaven, certainly has not the virtue, or what Theologians call the *Habitus* of faith. Montfort merely means that, as Our Lady has been commissioned to distribute to men all graces and heavenly gifts *(see* No. 25), so likewise, she, with the consent of the Most High, imparts to our faith the qualities of the faith she had on earth; for example, she makes our faith pure, lively, firm, active, etc.

3 That is, the hearts of the obdurate and the minds of the proud.

ARTICLE III.

Third Effect.—The grace of pure love.

215. (iii) This Mother of fair love[4] will lift from your heart all scruples and inordinate servile fear; she will open and enlarge it to run in the way of the commandments of her Son[5] with the holy freedom of the children of God, and fill it with the pure love of which she holds the treasury;[6] so that you will no longer act, as you have done, through fear of God who is Charity, but through pure love of Him. You will look upon Him as your loving Father, whom you will ever try to please and with whom you will converse confidently, as a child with its father. Should you have the misfortune to offend Him, you will at once humble yourself before Him and humbly beg His pardon; you will stretch out your hand to Him with simplicity and will rise from your sin, your heart full of love, neither troubled nor confused, and continue on your way to Him without discouragement.

ARTICLE IV.

Fourth Effect.—Great confidence in God and in Mary.

216. (iv) Our Blessed Lady will fill you with great confidence in God and in herself: (1) because you will no longer approach Jesus Christ by yourself, but always through this loving Mother; (2) because, as you have given her all your merits, graces and satisfactions to dispose of as she pleases, she will impart to you her virtues and clothe you in her merits so that you can say confidently to God: "Behold Mary Thy handmaid, be it done unto me according to Thy word." *Ecce*

---

4 Eccli, xxiv, 24.
5 Ps. cxviii, 32.
6 Cf. No. 169.

ancilla Domini, fiat mihi secundum verbum tuum.[7] (3) because, as you have given yourself entirely to her, body and soul, she, who is liberal with the liberal and more liberal even than the most liberal, will, in her turn, give herself to you in a marvellous but real manner, so that you can say boldly to her; *Tuus sum ego, salvum me fac*—"I am thine, O Blessed Virgin, save me";[8] or, like the beloved Disciple, as I have said previously,[9] *Accepi te in mea*—"I have taken thee, Blessed Mother, for my all." You may also say with St Bonaventure: *Ecce Domina salvatrix mea, fiducialiter agam, et non timebo, quia fortitudo mea et laus mea in Domino es tu;*[10] and elsewhere: *Tuus totus ego sum et omnia mea tua sunt: O Virgo gloriosa, super omnia benedicta, ponam te ut signaculum super cor meum, quia fortis est ut mors dilectio tua.*[11] "My loving and redeeming Mistress, I shall act with confidence and I shall not fear, because thou art my strength and praise in the Lord ... I am all thine and all that I have is thine; O glorious Virgin blessed above all things created; let me place thee as a seal upon my heart, for thy love is strong as death!" You can say to God with the sentiments of the prophet: *Domine, non est exaltatum cor, meum neque elati sunt oculi mei: neque ambulavi in magnis, neque in mirabilibus super me: si non humiliter sentiebam, sed exaitavi animam meam: sicut ablactatus est super matre sua, ita retributio in anima mea*[12]—"Lord, my heart is not exalted nor are my eyes lofty, neither have I walked in great matters nor in wonderful things above me; yet even in this I am not humble; but I have lifted up and encouraged my soul; I am as a child, weaned from earthly pleasures and resting on

---

7 Luke i, 38.
8 Ps. cxviii, 94.
9 Cf. No. 179.
10 Psalter Majus B.V.
11 Psalter Majus B.V.
12 Ps. cxxx, 1-2.

its mother's bosom; and it is upon this bosom that all good things come to me."

(4) What will still further increase your confidence in her is that, having given her in trust all the good which is in you, that she may dispose of it or keep it, you will have less confidence in yourself and much more in her, who is your treasury. Oh! what confidence and what consolation for a soul to be able to say that the Treasury of God, wherein he has placed all that He holds most precious, is its treasury also! *Ipsa est thesaurus Domini:* She is, says a saintly man, the treasury of the Lord.[13]

ARTICLE V.

Fifth Effect.—Communication of the soul and spirit of Mary.

217. (v) The soul of Mary will communicate itself to you to glorify the Lord. Her spirit will take the place of yours to rejoice in God, its Saviour, provided you are faithful to the practice of this devotion. *Sit in singulis anima Mariae ut magnificet Dominum; sit in singulis spiritus Mariae, ut exultet in Deo:*[14] "Let the soul of Mary be in each one to glorify the Lord, let the spirit of Mary be in each one to rejoice in God." Oh, when will that happy time come, asks a saintly man of our own day who was completely absorbed in Mary, when the divine Mary is set up in men's hearts as Mistress and Ruler, to subject them fully to the empire of the One Most High Jesus? When will souls breathe Mary as the body breathes air? When that time comes wondrous things will take place here below, for the Holy Ghost finding His beloved Spouse reproduced in souls will come upon them in abundance, filling them with

13 Idiota *(In contemplatione B. V.M.).*
14 St Ambrose *(Expositio in Luc.* Lib. ii, No. 26).

His gifts, particularly the gift of Wisdom, wherewith to work miracles of grace. My dear brother, when will that happy time come, the age of Mary, when many souls, chosen and obtained from the Most High by Mary, casting themselves completely into the abyss of her interior, will become the living copies of Mary, to love and glorify Jesus Christ? That time will come only when the devotion I teach is known and practised. *Ut adveniat regnum tuum, adveniat regnum Mariae.*[15]

ARTICLE VI.

Transformation of our souls into the image of Jesus Christ in the mould of Mary.

218. (vi) If Mary, who is the tree of life, is well cultivated in our soul by fidelity to the practices of this devotion, she will in due course bear fruit, and her fruit is none other than Jesus Christ. I see many devoted souls seeking Jesus Christ by one road or another; and often, when they have laboured much throughout the night, they can say: *Per totam noctem laborantes, nihil cepimus.*—"Though we have laboured all night, we have taken nothing."[16] To them we can say: *Laborastis multum, et intulistis parum*[17]—"You have laboured much, and gained little." Jesus Christ is still weak within you. But in the immaculate path of Mary and by the divine practice that I teach, we work by day, we work in a holy place, we labour but little. There is no night in Mary for in her there was no sin, no slightest shadow. Mary is a holy place, the Holy of Holies in which the saints are formed and moulded.

219. Please note that I say the saints are moulded in Mary. There is a vast difference between carving a statue, by blows of

---

15 "That Thy Kingdom may come, may the reign of Mary come."
16 Luke v, 5.
17 Aggeus i, 6. The real text is *Seminastis multum.*

hammer and chisel, and making a statue by casting it into a mould. Sculptors and statuaries labour much in making statues in the first manner and they need much time; but in the second manner they have little work and make them in a very short time. St Augustine calls Our Blessed Lady *forma Dei*— "the mould of God", *Si formam Dei te appellem, digna existis:*[18] She is the mould fit to form gods. He who is cast in this divine mould is soon formed and moulded in Jesus Christ, and Jesus Christ in him; with little cost and in little time he will become god-like, since he is cast in the same mould which formed a God.

220. I think I can very well compare those spiritual directors and devout persons who wish to form Jesus Christ in themselves and in others by methods other than this, with sculptors who, relying on their own knowledge, their skill and their art, chip away endlessly with hammer and chisel at hard stone or badly polished wood, in an effort to form an image of Jesus Christ. Sometimes they do not reproduce a true likeness of Jesus Christ, either through lack of knowledge and experience of the person of Jesus Christ, or because of some clumsy blow which spoils the whole work. But as for those who accept this secret of grace which I offer them, I would rightly compare them to founders and moulders who having discovered the beautiful mould of Mary, wherein Jesus Christ was naturally and divinely formed, rely not on their own skill but on the excellence of the mould, and cast and abandon themselves in Mary to become the true images of Jesus Christ.

221. Oh, beautiful and true comparison! But who will comprehend it? I would that you might, my dear brother. But remember that only molten and liquid substances are cast into a mould; which means that you must break up and melt down

---

18   Sermo 208. "Thou art worthy to be called the mould of God." (Inter, opp. St Augustini.)

the old Adam in you in order to become like unto the New One[19] in Mary.

ARTICLE VII.

The greater glory of Jesus Christ.

222. (vii) By this devotion, faithfully observed, you will give more glory to Jesus Christ in a month than by any other, however difficult, in many years. And here are my reasons for this statement.

(1) Because, performing all your actions through the Blessed Virgin, as this devotion teaches, you abandon your own intentions, good and known to you though they may be, and lose yourself, so to speak, in those of Our Blessed Lady, although you do not know them. In this way, you participate in the sublimity of her intentions which were so pure that she gave greater glory to God by the least of her actions—twirling her distaff, or a single stitch—than St Laurence by his cruel martyrdom on the gridiron; more even than all the saints in their most heroic actions. Hence it is that during her sojourn on earth she acquired such a superabundance of merits and graces that it would be easier to count the stars in heaven, the drops in the ocean or the sands of the shore, than to count her merits and graces; hence it is that she gave more glory to God than all the angels and saints have given or will give.

Oh Mary, what a prodigy art thou! Thou canst work but prodigies in souls that abandon themselves entirely to thee.

223. (2) Because by this devotion, the soul, counting as nothing its own thoughts and actions, relying only on the dispositions of Mary in approaching and even speaking to Jesus, shows far more humility than other souls who act of themselves and imperceptibly rely on and are pleased with their

19 Eph. iv, 22-24.

own dispositions; consequently, that soul gives greater glory to God who is perfectly glorified only by the meek and humble of heart.

224. (3) Because Our Blessed Lady, who, in her immense love, deigns to receive into her virginal hands the offering of our actions, imparts to them an admirable beauty and lustre. She offers them herself to Jesus Christ; and there can be no doubt that Our Lord is more glorified thereby than if we offered them with our own sinful hands.

225. (4) Lastly, because you never think of Mary, without Mary thinking of God in your stead; you never praise or honour Mary, without Mary praising and honouring God with you. Mary is altogether relative to God; indeed, I would call her the relation to God, who exists only because of God; she is the echo of God, who speaks and repeats only God; if you say "Mary", she says "God". St Elizabeth praised Mary and called her blessed, because she had believed; Mary the faithful echo of God, sang: *Magnificat anima mea Dominum*—"My soul doth magnify the Lord."[20] What Mary did then, she now does day by day. When she is praised, when she is loved or honoured, when she is presented with anything, God is praised, God is honoured and loved, and through Mary and in Mary God receives the gift.

---

20 Luke i, 46.

CHAPTER EIGHT.

SPECIAL PRACTICES OF THIS DEVOTION.

ARTICLE I.

Exterior Practices.

226. Although this devotion is essentially interior[1] it is not lacking in exterior practices which are not to be neglected: *Haec oportuit facere et ilia non omittere.*[2] This is so, because external practices, properly performed, help the interior ones; because man, who is always led by his senses, is reminded by such practices of what he is doing or should do; and also because they tend to edify those who witness them, which purely internal practices cannot do. And let no worldling or critic here interfere to proclaim that true devotion is in the heart; that externals must be avoided, that they can spring from vanity, that devotion must be hidden, etc. With my Master I reply to them "Let men see your good works that they may glorify your Father who is in heaven."[3] As St Gregory points out, this does not mean that they should indulge in exterior practices and devotion to please men or to attract their praise,[4] this would be vanity; but such actions are sometimes performed before men with the intention of pleasing God and glorifying Him, without caring for the contempt or praise of mankind.

I shall briefly mention some exterior practices that I call exterior not because they are performed without inward intention, but because they really have an exterior side to them, as distinct from the purely interior.

---

1 Cf. No. 119.
2 Mat. xxiii, 23.
3 Mat. v, 16.
4 Homilia II in Evang.

1. The Consecration and its preparatory Exercises.

227. *First practice.*—Those who desire to take up this special devotion which is not erected into a Confraternity, though such is to be wished,[5] having spent twelve days at least, as I said in the first part of this preparation for the reign of Jesus Christ, in ridding themselves of the spirit of the world, which is opposed to the spirit of Jesus Christ, should during three weeks fill themselves with the spirit of Jesus Christ, through the Most Blessed Virgin.[6] Here is the order they should follow:—

228. During the first week, they will say all their prayers and perform their acts of devotion to obtain knowledge of themselves and contrition of their sins, and for the same end they should do all their actions in a spirit of humility. They may, if they please, meditate on what I have said about our corrupt nature, and consider themselves during the six days of the week as snails, slugs, toads, swine, serpents, and goats; or else they may meditate on these three considerations of St Bernard: *Cogita quid fueris, semen putridum; quid sis, vas stercorum; quid futurus sis, esca vermium.*[7] They will ask Our Lord and the Holy Ghost to enlighten them, saying: *Domine, ut videam;*[8] or *Noverim me;*[9] or *Veni Sancte Spiritus,* and every day they will recite the Litany of the Holy Ghost, with the prayer that follows as indicated in the first part of this work. They will have recourse to Our Blessed Lady and beg her to obtain for them this great grace which is the foundation of others,

5 De Montfort's wish was realised in 1913, when the Archconfraternity of Mary, Queen of our hearts, was canonically erected in Rome. It now has over 80 centres throughout the world.

6 These words of De Montfort seem to allude to another work of his which might have served as an Introduction to the True Devotion. Perhaps he means *L'Amour de la Sagesse Eternelle,* well known in France.

7 "Remember what thou wert: a little slime; what thou art: a putrid vessel; what thou shalt be; the food of worms."

8 Luke xviii, 41: "Lord, that I may see."

9 St Augustine. "That I may know myself."

and for that purpose, they will say each day *Ave Maris Stella,* and the Litany of the Blessed Virgin.

229. During the second week, in all their prayers and works each day, they will strive to acquire the knowledge of the Most Blessed Virgin. They will ask this knowledge of the Holy Ghost, and should read and meditate what we have said about her. As during the first week, they will recite daily the Litany of the Holy Ghost and the *Ave Maris Stella,* and in addition say a Rosary, or at least a Chaplet of five decades, for this intention.

230. During the third week they will strive to obtain the knowledge of Jesus Christ. They may read and meditate on what we have said about Him, and recite the prayer of St Augustine which they will find towards the beginning of this second part[10]. With the same Saint, they can constantly repeat, *Noverim Te,* "Lord, that I may know Thee!" or *Domine, ut videam.* "Lord, that I may see who Thou art!" They will recite, as during the preceding weeks, the Litany of the Holy Ghost and the *Ave Maris Stella,* and add to this every day the Litanies of Jesus.

231. At the end of the three weeks, they will go to confession and receive Holy Communion, with the intention of consecrating themselves to Jesus Christ as His slaves of love, by the hands of Mary. After Holy Communion, for which they should follow the method given later, they will recite the Act of their Consecration which is given at the end of this work; they ought to copy it or have it copied, unless they have a printed copy, and they should sign it on the same day.

232. It would be a good thing on that day to pay some tribute to Jesus Christ and His Blessed Mother, either as a penance for their past unfaithfulness to the promises of their Baptism, or in testimony of their dependence on the sovereignty

---

10 Cf. No. 67.

of Jesus and Mary. Now such tribute should be in proportion to each one's means and devotion; for example, fasting, mortification, almsgiving, a votive candle; were they to give but a pin as homage, if it were given with a good heart, it would be enough for Jesus, who considers only one's good will.

233. Once a year at least, on the anniversary, they should renew this same consecration, and observe the same practices for three weeks. They might also renew it every month, and even every day, by these few words: *Tuus totus ego sum, et omnia mea tua sunt.* "*I* am all thine, and all that I have is thine," O my loving Jesus through Mary, Thy Holy Mother[11].

2. Recitation of the Little Crown of the Blessed Virgin.

234. *Second practice.* They should recite every day of their lives, without however inconveniencing themselves, the Little Crown of the Blessed Virgin, composed of three Our Fathers and twelve Hail Marys in honour of the twelve privileges and grandeurs of the Blessed Virgin. This devotion is very old arid is founded on Scripture. St John saw a woman crowned with twelve stars, clothed with the sun and having the moon beneath her feet;[12] and this woman, according to the interpreters,[13] is the Most Blessed Virgin.

235. There are many ways of saying this Little Crown well; but it would be too long to mention them here; the Holy Ghost will teach those who are most faithful to this devotion. However, to recite it quite simply, we begin by: *Dignare me laudare te, Virgo sacrata; Da mihi virtutem contra hostes tuos;*[14] next recite the *Credo;* and then a *Pater* and four *Aves,* followed

---

11   The members of the Archconfraternity can gain an indulgence of 300 days each time they renew their consecration with these words: *I am all Thine and all I have I offer Thee, O my loving Jesus, through Mary, Thy most holy Mother.*

12   Apoc. xii, 1.

13   Among others, St Augustine and St Bernard.

14   Office of Our Lady at Vespers: "Vouchsafe that I may praise thee, O Virgin most holy; give me strength against thy enemies."

by one *Gloria Patri;* and so on to the end. In conclusion the *Sub tuum praesidium* is said.

3. The wearing of little iron chains.

236. *Third practice.* It is very praiseworthy, glorious and useful for those who have thus become the slaves of Jesus in Mary to wear, in token of their loving slavery, some little chain that has been blessed for this special purpose.[15] It is perfectly true that these external signs are not essential, and a person who has embraced this devotion may very well dispense with them; nevertheless, I cannot refrain from warmly praising those who, having shaken off the shameful chains of the slavery of the devil, in which original sin and perhaps actual sins bound them, willingly take upon themselves the glorious slavery of Jesus Christ and with St Paul glory in the chains they wear for Christ[16]—chains more glorious and precious far, though they are but coarse iron, than all the golden chains of emperors.

237. Once there was nothing more infamous than the Cross, and now that rood is the most glorious boast of Christendom. We may say the same of the chains of slavery. There was nothing more ignominious among the ancients, nothing more shameful among the heathens even to this day; but among Christians there is nothing more glorious than the chains of Jesus Christ, because they deliver us and preserve us from the shameful bonds of sin and the devil. They set us free and bind us to Jesus and Mary, not by compulsion or force like galley-slaves, but by charity and love, like children: *Traham eos in vinculis caritatis* (Osee XI, 4). "I shall draw them to

---

15 It has been said that the wearing of such chains is forbidden by the Roman Congregations. But there is nothing in their Decrees forbidding the use of these chains, if worn as a sign of our voluntary slavery of Jesus in Mary, according to De Montfort's counsel. (Cf. Analecta Juris Pontificii. First Series. Col. 757.)

16 Eph. iii, 1; Phil. 9.

me", said God by the mouth of the prophet, "by the chains of love"; consequently they are strong as death,[17] even stronger, for those who wear these glorious signs faithfully till death. For, though death will destroy their body by reducing it to dust, it will not destroy the chains of their slavery, which, being of iron, do not so easily perish; and perhaps on the day of their resurrection, at the great last Judgment, these chains, still clinging to their bones, will become part of their glory, and be changed into chains of light and splendour. Happy then, a thousand times, are the illustrious slaves of Jesus in Mary, who carry their chains even to the grave!

238. Here are the reasons for wearing the little chains:— (i) To remind the Christian of the vows and promises of his Baptism, and their perfect renewal made by this devotion, and his strict obligation of remaining faithful to them. As man, who acts more frequently according to the senses than by pure faith, easily forgets his duties towards God, if he has no exterior sign to remind him of them, these little chains are to him a wonderful reminder of the bonds of sin and of the slavery of the devil, from which Baptism has freed him; and at the same time they remind him of his dependence on Jesus, vowed in Baptism and ratified by the renewal of his vows. One of the reasons why so many Christians do not think of their baptismal vows, and live with as much licence as if, like the heathens, they had promised nothing to God, is that they do not wear any external sign to remind them of these vows.

239. (ii) To show that we are not ashamed of the slavery and servitude of Jesus Christ, and that we renounce the baneful slavery of the world, of sin and of the devil.

(iii) To shield and preserve us from the chains of sin and of the devil. For we must wear either the chains of sin, or the

---

17 Cant, viii, 6.

chains of charity and salvation: *Vinculo, peccatorum; in vinculis charitatis.*[18]

240. Ah! my dear brother, let us break the chains of sin and of sinners, of the world and of worldlings, of the devil and his ministers; and cast far from us their deadly yoke: *Dirumpamus vincula, eorum, et projiciamus a nobis jugum ipsorum;*[19] and, to use the words of the Holy Ghost, let us put our feet into His glorious fetters, and our neck into His chains: *Irijice pedem tuum in compedes illius, et in torques illius collum tuum* (Eccl. VI). Let us bow down our shoulders and bear Wisdom, who is Jesus Christ, and we shall not be grieved with His bonds: *Subjice humerum tuum et porta illam, et ne acedieris vinculis ejus* (Eccl. VI). Notice how, before these words the Holy Ghost prepares the soul for them, lest it should reject His important counsel: *Audi, fili, accipe consilium intellectus, et ne abjicias consilium meum.*—Hearken, my son, and receive a counsel of understanding, and reject not my counsel. (Eccl. VI.)

241. Allow me here, my dear friend, to join with the Holy Ghost, in giving you the same counsel: *Vincula illius alligatura salutaris.*[20] "His chains are chains of salvation." As Jesus Christ on the Cross must draw all men to Himself, whether they will it or not, He will draw the reprobate by the fetters of their sins, to enchain them like galley-slaves and devils to His eternal anger and avenging justice; but the predestinate He will draw, and especially in these latter days, by the chains of love: *Omnia traham ad meipsum*[21]—*traham eos in vinculis charitatis* (Osee XI, 4).

242. These loving slaves or bondmen of Jesus Christ, *vincti Christi,*[22] can carry their chains around the neck, on the

---

18 Osee. xi, 4.
19 Ps. ii, 3.
20 Eccli. vi, 31.
21 John xii, 32.
22 Eph. iii, 1.

arms, around the loins or on their feet. Fr. Vincent Caraffa, seventh General of the Society of Jesus, who died in the odour of sanctity in 1643, carried as a token of slavery an iron ring on his feet and was wont to say that his great regret was that he could not publicly drag a chain. Mother Agnes of Jesus, of whom we have already spoken,[23] wore an iron chain around the waist. Others have worn it around the neck as a penance for the necklaces of pearls they wore in the world; still others have worn it on their arm, to remind them in their manual work that they are the slaves of Christ.

4. Special devotion to the mystery of the Incarnation.

243. *Fourth practice.* Loving slaves of Jesus in Mary should have a special devotion to the great mystery of the Incarnation of the Word, March 25,[24] which is the mystery proper to this devotion, for it was inspired by the Holy Ghost: (i) to honour and imitate the ineffable dependence on Mary adopted by God the Son, for the glory of His Father and our salvation. This divine dependence shines forth especially in this mystery, where Jesus is a captive and a slave in the womb of His divine Mother and depends on her for all things: (ii) to thank God for the incomparable graces He has bestowed on Mary and more particularly for having chosen her to be His most Worthy Mother, which choice was made in this mystery. These are the two principal ends of the slavery of Jesus in Mary.

244. Please note that I usually say: *The slave of Jesus in Mary; the slavery of Jesus in Mary,* We can truly say, as some have already done,[25] *the slave of Mary; the slavery of the Blessed Virgin;* but I think it better to say *the slave of Jesus in Mary.* This was the advice given by M. Tronson, Superior General

---

23 Cf. No. 170.

24 On March 25th, feast of the Annunciation, members of the Archconfraternity can gain a Plenary Indulgence.

25 Thus H. M. Boudon in his book mentioned in No. 159

of St Sulpice, renowned for rare prudence and consummate piety, when he was consulted by a certain ecclesiastic.

Here are the reasons for it:—

245. Firstly, as we are living in an age of pride, when a great number of puffed-up scholars, of self-reliant and critical minds find fault with the best established and most solid practices of piety, it is better to speak of *the Slavery of Jesus in Mary,* and to call oneself *the slave of Jesus Christ* rather than *the slave of Mary,* so as to avoid giving any unnecessary opportunity for criticism. We thus take the name of this devotion from its ultimate end, Jesus Christ, rather than from the way and the means to achieve this end, which is Mary; although in all truth we can very well use one or the other without any scruple, as I myself do. For example, a man who is going from Orleans to Tours, by way of Amboise, can quite truthfully say that he is going to Amboise and that he is going to Tours, that he is a traveller to Amboise and a traveller to Tours, but with this difference: Amboise is just his direct road to Tours, and only Tours is his ultimate end and the terminus of his journey.

246. Secondly, as the principal mystery celebrated and honoured in this devotion is the mystery of the Incarnation, wherein we find Jesus only in Mary, incarnate in her womb, it is more fitting to say: *the slavery of Jesus in Mary,* of Jesus living and reigning in Mary, according to the beautiful prayer of so many great men: "O Jesus, living in Mary, come and dwell in us in the spirit of Thy sanctity, etc."

247. Thirdly, this manner of speaking expresses better the intimate union that exists between Jesus and Mary. So intimately are they united that one is wholly in the other: Jesus is wholly in Mary, and Mary is wholly in Jesus; or rather, she no longer is, but Jesus alone is in her; light could be more easily separated from the sun than Mary from Jesus. So that we can call Our Lord *"Jesus of Mary"* and the Blessed Virgin *"Mary of Jesus"*.

248. As I have no time to pause here and give an explanation of the excellences and grandeurs of the mystery of Jesus living and reigning in Mary, or the Incarnation of the Word, I shall content myself with these following brief statements: The Incarnation is the first mystery of Jesus Christ, the most hidden, the most exalted and the least known. In this mystery, in the womb of Mary—called by the saints for that reason *Aula Sacramentorum*,[26] House of God's secrets—and together with her, Jesus chose all His elect. Jesus worked all subsequent mysteries of His Life by accepting them in this mystery: *Jesus ingrediens in mundum dicit: Ecce venio ut faciam, Deus, voluntatem tuam.*[27] Consequently, this mystery is an abridgement of all mysteries, containing as it does the will and grace of them all. Lastly, this mystery is the throne of the mercy, the liberality, and the glory of God. For us it is the throne of His mercy, for, since we can approach Jesus only through Mary, we cannot see or speak to Him without her intervention. There, ever heedful of the prayers of His Beloved Mother, Jesus always grants grace and mercy to poor sinners. *Adeamus ergo cum fiducia ad thronum gratiae.*[28] For Mary it is the throne of His liberality for, whilst the new Adam dwelt in this true earthly paradise, God performed then so many latent marvels that neither angels nor men have any comprehension of them. For this reason the saints call Mary the magnificence of God: *Magnificentia Dei*[29] as if God were magnificent only in Mary; *solummodo ibi magnificus Dominus*[30] For His Father it is the throne of His glory, for it was in Mary that Jesus Christ perfectly appeased His Father, angered with mankind; that He perfectly restored the glory ravished from Him by sin. It was

---

26 St Ambrose: *De Instit. Virg.* Chap. vii, 50.
27 Heb.x, 5-9.
28 Heb.iv, 16.
29 Cf. No. 6.
30 Is. xxxiii, 21.

in Mary that, by His sacrifice of self and of His own will, He gave more glory to God than would have given all the sacrifices of the Old Law, and finally gave Him an infinite glory which He had never yet received from men.

5. A great devotion to the Hail Mary and the Rosary.

249. *Fifth practice.* Those who adopt this devotion should have a great devotion to the Hail Mary (the Angelical Salutation), of which few Christians, however enlightened, understand the value, the merit, the excellence and the necessity. Our Blessed Lady herself had to appear on different occasions to great and enlightened saints, such as St Dominic, St John Capistran, and Blessed Alan de Rupe, to bring home to them the realisation of its value. They composed whole books relating the wonders worked and the efficacy of this prayer in the conversion of souls. They loudly proclaimed and publicly preached that just as the salvation of the world began with the Hail Mary so the salvation of each individual soul was linked up with this prayer; that this prayer brought to a dry and sterile world the Fruit of Life; and that this same prayer, well said, will make the word of God germinate in our soul and bring forth Jesus Christ the Fruit of Life. They tell us also that the Hail Mary is the heavenly dew which waters the earth of our soul to make it bring forth its fruit in due season; and that the soul which is not watered by this prayer, by this heavenly dew, bears no fruit, but rather thorns and brambles, and is ripe for the curse of God.[31]

250. Here is what Our Lady revealed to Blessed Alan de Rupe, as he has recorded in his book on the dignity of the Rosary: *De Dignitate Rosarii,* and has since been recorded by Cartagena: "Know, my son, and make known to all that it is a probable and proximate sign of eternal damnation to be filled

---

31 Heb. vi, 8.

with dislike, to be lukewarm or negligent in saying the Angelical Salutation, by which the whole world was restored."
Scias enim et secure intelligas et inde late omnibus patefacias,
quod videlicet signum probabile est et propinquum aeternae
damnationis horrere et acediari ac negligere salutationem an-
gelicam, totius mundi reparationem (Lib. de Dignit. Rosarii,
Cap. II). These are words at once terrible and consoling, and
we should find it hard to believe them had we not the testimony of this saintly man, of St Dominic before him, and of
many great men since, together with the experience of many
centuries. For it has always been a notable fact that those
who bear the sign of reprobation as do all heretics, the ungodly, the proud and the lovers of the world, hate or despise
the *Hail Mary* and the Rosary. Heretics still learn and recite
the *Our Father*, but not the *Hail Mary* or the Rosary; they
hold it in abhorrence and would sooner carry a snake than a
Rosary. The proud also, though Catholics, because they have
the same inclinations as their father Lucifer, despise or are
indifferent towards the *Hail Mary*, looking on the Rosary as
an old woman's devotion, good only for the ignorant and the
illiterate. On the other hand, experience demonstrates that
those who show striking signs of predestination, love and appreciate the *Hail Mary*, reciting it with joy; the closer they are
to God, the more do they love this prayer. This, also is what
Our Blessed Lady told Alan de Rupe after having said the
words I have just quoted.

251. Why or how it should be so I cannot say, but it is
perfectly true that I have no better secret of knowing if a person belongs to God than to find out if he likes to say the *Hail*
Mary and the Rosary. I say "if he likes," for it may well be
that some are prevented from saying it by a natural or even
supernatural cause; nevertheless he loves it always and induces
others to say it.

252. PREDESTINATE SOULS, SLAVES OF JESUS IN MARY, know that after the *Our Father,* the *Hail Mary* is the most beautiful of prayers. It is the most perfect compliment that you can pay to Mary, for it is the compliment paid through an Archangel by the Most High God in order to win her heart. So mighty was its effect upon her heart, through the secret charms in which it abounds, that despite her profound humility she gave her consent to the Incarnation. If you say it as it should be said, this compliment will infallibly gain you her heart.

253. When it is well said, that is, with attention, devotion and dignity, the *Hail Mary* is, according to the saints, the enemy of the devil which puts him to flight, the hammer that crushes him, the sanctification of the soul, the joy of angels, the hymn of the predestinate, the canticle of the New Testament, the delight of Mary and the glory of the Most Blessed Trinity. The *Hail Mary* is the dew from heaven that brings fertility to the soul, it is the chaste and loving kiss we give to Mary, the crimson rose we present to her, the precious pearl we offer her, the cup of ambrosia, of divine nectar, that we give her. Such, are the comparisons of the Saints.

254. I earnestly beg you then, by the love I bear you in Jesus and Mary, not to be content with reciting the Little Crown of the Blessed Virgin, but also to say a Chaplet and even, if time permits, the whole Rosary of fifteen decades each day. At the hour of death you will bless the day and hour when you hearkened to my words, and after having sown in the blessings of Jesus and Mary you will reap eternal blessings in heaven. *Qui seminat in benedictionibus, de benedictionibus et metet.*[32]

6. *The recitation of the Magnificat.*

255. *Sixth practice.*—To thank God for the graces He has given to Our Lady, her slaves will often say the *Magnificat,*

---

32 2 Cor. ix, 6.

following the example of Blessed Mary D'Oignies and several other Saints. It is the only prayer, the only hymn composed by the Blessed Virgin, or rather by Jesus in her, as it was He who spoke through her mouth. It is the greatest offering of praise that God ever received under the law of grace. On the one hand, it is the most humble and thankful, on the other, the most sublime and lofty of all hymns. In it are contained mysteries so great and so hidden that the angels themselves cannot comprehend them. The pious and learned Gerson, having spent the greater part of his life in composing on the most difficult subjects treatises overflowing with erudition and piety, turned with trembling at the end of his life to the explanation of the Magnificat wherewith to crown all his other works. He tells us in a folio volume which he composed on the subject many wonderful things concerning this beautiful and divine canticle. Among other things he tells us that the Most Blessed Virgin herself frequently recited it, particularly as thanksgiving after Holy Communion. The learned Benzonius in his explanation of this prayer relates many miracles operated by its power and states that, trembling, the devils take to flight when they hear these words of the Magnificat: *Fecit potentiam in brachio suo, dispersit superbos mente cordis sui.*[33]

7. Contempt of the world.

256. *Seventh practice.*—The faithful slaves of Mary must greatly despise, hate and shun this corrupt world, and make use of the practices of contempt of the world which we have given in the first part of this treatise.[34]

---

33 Luke i, 51: "He hath shown might in his arm; he hath scattered the proud in the conceit of their heart."
34 Cf. footnote to No. 227.

ARTICLE II.

Particular and interior practices for those who wish to be perfect.

257. Besides the exterior practices of this devotion, of which I have just spoken and which are not to be omitted from motives of contempt or neglect, but practised in so far as the state and condition of each one permit, here are some very sanctifying interior practices for those whom the Holy Ghost calls to a high degree of perfection.

They can be expressed in four words: to do all our actions *through Mary, with Mary, in Mary* and *for Mary,* so as to perform them, more perfectly *through Jesus, with Jesus, in Jesus* and *for Jesus.*

1. Through Mary.

258. We should do our actions through Mary, that is, we should obey her in all things and allow ourselves to be led by her spirit, which is the Holy Spirit of God. Those who are led by the Spirit of God are the children of God: *Qui spiritu Dei aguntur, ii sunt filii Dei.*[35] Those who are led by the spirit of Mary, are the children of Mary, and consequently children of God, as we have explained;[36] and among the many devotees of Our Blessed Lady, only those who are led by her spirit are truly and faithfully devoted to her. I have said that the spirit of Mary is the Spirit of God, because she was never led by her own spirit, but always by the Spirit of God, who possessed her so completely that He has become her own spirit.

It is on account of this that St Ambrose says: *Sit in singulis,* etc. "Let the soul of Mary be in each one of us to magnify the Lord; and the spirit of Mary be in each one of us to re-

---

35 Rom. viii, 14.
36 Cf. Nos. 29-30.

joice in God."[37] How happy is the soul which, like the good Jesuit brother Rodriguez, who died in the odour of sanctity,[38] is completely possessed and governed by the spirit of Mary, a spirit that is gentle yet strong, zealous yet prudent, humble yet courageous, pure yet fruitful.

259. The soul that wishes to be led by this spirit of Mary should (i) renounce its own spirit, its own views and its own will before doing anything, for example, before meditation, before saying or hearing Mass, before Communion, etc., because the darkness of our own spirit, the malice of our own will and operations, although appearing good to us, would hinder the holy spirit of Mary, were we to follow them, (ii) We should give ourselves up to the spirit of Mary in order to be moved and directed in the way she desires. We should place and leave ourselves in her virginal hands, like an instrument in the hands of a craftsman, or a lute in the hands of an artist. Like a stone thrown into the sea we should lose and abandon ourselves in her. This is done simply and in an instant, by a flash of the mind, a slight movement of the will; or it can be done verbally, by saying, for example: *"I renounce myself, I give myself to you, my Blessed Mother."* It may well be that we shall feel no noticeable sweetness in this act of union, but it is none the less real; just as if we were to say—which God forbid—"I give myself to the devil," with equal sincerity. Although this were said with no perceptible change, we should none the less truly belong to the devil, (iii) From time to time, during an action and after it, we should renew this same act of offering and of union; the more we do so, the sooner shall we be sanctified and the sooner reach union with Christ, which is the necessary sequel to union with Mary, since the spirit of Mary is the spirit of Jesus.

---

37 Cf. No. 217.
38 Canonised by Leo xiii in 1888.

2. With Mary.

260. We should perform our actions with Mary; that is to say, in all our actions we should look upon Mary as the accomplished model of all virtue and perfection, fashioned by the Holy Ghost in a mere creature, for us to imitate as far as our limited capacity allows us. In every action therefore we should consider how Mary has done it, or how she would do it if she were in our place. For this reason we must examine and meditate on the great virtues she practised during her life-time, particularly, (1) her lively faith, by which she believed without hesitation the word of the angel. To the very foot of the Cross on Calvary, she believed faithfully and constantly; (2) her deep humility, which made her hide herself, remain silent, submit herself in all things and place herself last; (3) her divine purity, which never has had nor ever will have an equal under Heaven; and so on for all her other virtues.

Be it well remembered, I repeat a second time, that Mary is the great and unique mould of God,[39] fitted to make living images of Him at little cost and in a short time; remember also that a soul which finds this mould and casts itself therein is rapidly transformed into Jesus Christ, who is truly reproduced by it.

3. In Mary.

261. We should do all our actions in Mary.

To understand this practice thoroughly, we must know that Our Lady is the true earthly paradise of the new Adam, and that the first Eden was but a figure of her. There are, then, in this earthly paradise, riches, beauties, rarities and inexplicable delights, which the new Adam, Jesus Christ, has left there. In this paradise He took His delight for nine months, worked His wonders, and displayed His riches with

---

39 Cf. No. 218.

the magnificence of a God. This most holy place is made up
of only virgin and immaculate soil from which was formed
and nourished the new Adam without spot or stain, by the
operation of the Holy Ghost who dwells therein. In this
earthly paradise grows the true tree of life which bore Jesus
Christ, the Fruit of Life; there is the tree of the knowledge
of good and evil, which gave light to the world. In this divine spot there are trees planted by the hand of God and
watered by His divine unction, which have borne and daily
bear fruit of divine taste; there are flowerbeds studded with
the beautiful and varied flowers of virtue spreading an odour
which delights even the Angels. There are meadows verdant
with hope; impregnable keeps; charming palaces of confidence, etc. The Holy Ghost alone can make known the truth
hidden behind these material figures. In this place the air is
pure, without infection, in this place there is no night, but
only the radiant day of the Sacred Humanity, the unshad-
owed sun of the Divinity. Here is to be found the ever burning furnace of charity, in which base metal is burnt up and
changed into gold. From the earth gushes a river of humility which dividing into four branches waters that enchanted
spot; these are the four cardinal virtues.

262. By the mouth of the Fathers, the Holy Ghost also
calls Mary (i) the Eastern Gate, through which, in this world,
the High Priest, Jesus Christ, enters and goes forth;[40] through
this gate, He first entered, and He will use it for His second
coming. (ii) The Sanctuary of the Divinity, the Dwelling Place
of the Blessed Trinity, the Throne of God, the City of God, the
Altar of God, the Temple of God, the World of God. All these
various epithets and titles are very real, referring to the different wonders and graces which the Most High has wrought in
Mary. Oh! what riches! what glory! what joy! what happiness

40   Ezech. xliv, 2-3.

to be able to enter and dwell in Mary, where the Most High has set up the throne of His supreme glory!

263. But how difficult it is for sinners such as we are to have the permission, the ability and the light to enter a spot so high and so holy; a spot guarded not by a cherub, as was the first earthly paradise,[41] but by the Holy Ghost Himself, who has made Himself absolute master of it and says of her: *Hortus conclusus, soror mea sponsa, hortus conclusus, fons signatus.*[42] Mary is enclosed, Mary is sealed. The wretched children of Adam and Eve, driven from the earthly paradise, can enter this new Paradise only by a special grace of the Holy Ghost, which they must merit.

264. After we have obtained this singular grace by our fidelity, we must dwell in the fair interior of Mary with joy, rest there peacefully, rely on her confidently, hide there with assurance and lose ourselves there without reserve, so that on her virginal bosom: (i) the soul may be nourished with the milk of her grace and her maternal tenderness; (ii) it may be delivered from its troubles, fears and scruples; (iii) it may be safe from all its enemies, the devil, the world and sin, who have never had entrance there; this is why Mary says that they who work in her shall not sin: *Qui operantur in me non peccabunt;*[43] that is, those who dwell in spirit in Our Blessed Lady will never fall into grievous sin; (iv) the soul may be formed in Jesus Christ and Jesus Christ in the soul; because her bosom is, as the Fathers say,[44] the House of the divine Secrets, where Jesus and all the elect have been formed: *Homo et homo natus est in ea.*[45]

---

41 Gen. iii, 24.
42 Cant, iv, 12: "My sister, my spouse, is a garden enclosed, a garden enclosed, a fountain sealed up."
43 Eccli. xxiv, 30.
44 Cf. No. 248.
45 Ps. lxxxvi, 5; Cf. No. 32.

4. For Mary.

265. We should, finally, perform all our actions for Mary, for as we have given ourselves entirely to her service it is but just that we should act towards her as a servant and slave. This does not mean that we take her as the ultimate end of such services, for that end is Jesus Christ alone. But we take her as our proximate end, our mysterious intermediary and the easy way of going to Him. Thus, as good servants and slaves, we must not remain idle but relying on her protection we must undertake and carry through great things for this august Sovereign. We should defend her privileges when they are questioned, we should uphold her glory when it is attacked. We should, if possible, draw every one to her service and to this true and solid devotion. We should speak out and thunder against those who misuse devotion to her in order to outrage her Son, and at the same time we must establish this true devotion. But we should claim from her for these little services no other reward than the honour of belonging to so beloved a Princess and the happiness of being united through her to Jesus her Son, by a bond that is indissoluble in time and in eternity.

GLORY BE TO JESUS IN MARY!
GLORY BE TO MARY IN JESUS!
GLORY BE TO GOD ALONE!

Supplement

How to practise this devotion in holy communion.

1. Before Holy Communion.

266. (i) Humble yourself profoundly before God. (ii) Renounce your own corrupt nature and your own dispositions, however good self-esteem might make them appear. (iii) Renew your consecration saying: *Tuus totus ego sum et omnia mea tua sunt*: "I am all thine, my dearest Mistress, and all that I have is thine." (iv) Beg this loving Mother to lend you her own heart,[1] that you may receive her Son with her dispositions. Remind her that her Son's glory requires that He should not come into a heart so stained and fickle as your own, which could not fail to diminish His glory and might perhaps lose Him. Tell her that if she will take up her dwelling in you to receive her Son, which she can do because of the dominion she holds over our hearts, He will be well received by her without stain and without danger of being outraged or lost: *Deus in medio ejus non commovebitur.*[2] Tell her with confidence that all you have given her of your goods does little to honour her, but that by your Holy Communion you wish to make her the same gift as was given her by the Eternal Father, and that thus she will be more honoured than if you had given her all the riches of this world. Tell her finally, that Jesus, whose love for her is unique, wishes still to take His delight and His repose in her, even though it be in your soul, dirtier and poorer than the stable to which Jesus willingly came because she was there. With these tender words beg her to lend you her heart: *Accipio te in mea omnia. Praebe mihi cor tuum, O Maria.*[3]

---

1 That is, the dispositions of her heart.
2 Ps. xlv, 6.
3 "O Mary, I take thee as my all; give me thy heart."

2. At Holy Communion.

267. As the time to receive Jesus approaches, after the *Pater Noster*, say thrice to Him: *Domine, non sum dignus*, etc. The first time as if you were telling the Eternal Father that, because of your evil thoughts and your ingratitude to so good a Father, you are not worthy to receive His only Son, but that here is Mary, His handmaid, *Ecce ancilla Domini*, who acts for you and who inspires you with singular confidence and hope in His Divine Majesty: *Quoniam singulariter in spe constituisti me.*[4]

268. To God the Son say: *Domine non sum dignus*, etc., that you are not worthy to receive Him because of idle and evil words and because of infidelity in His service; but that in spite of this you beg His pity, for you will lead Him to the house of His Mother and yours, nor will you let Him go till He has made it His dwelling place: *Tenui eum nec dimittam donec introducam illum in domum matris meae, et in cubiculum genitricis meae.*[5] Implore Him to rise and come to the place of His repose and the ark of His sanctification: *Surge Domine, in requiem tuam, tu et arca sanctificationis tuae.*[6] Tell him that unlike Esau you place no trust in your own merits, strength and preparation, but only in those of Mary your beloved Mother, just as Jacob trusted the diligence of his mother Rebecca. Tell Him that sinner and Esau though you are, still you dare to approach His Sanctity, supported and adorned with the merits and virtues of His Blessed Mother.

269. To the Holy Ghost say: *Domine non sum digitus*, etc., that because of your tepidity and wickedness of action, your resistance to His inspirations, you are not worthy to receive the Masterpiece of His Love, but that your confidence

4 Ps.iv, 10.
5 Cant, iii, 4.
6 Ps. cxxxi, 8.

is Mary, His faithful Spouse. Say with St Bernard: *Haec mea maxima fiducia est; haec tota ratio spei meae.*[7] You can even implore Him to overshadow Mary, His indissoluble Spouse, once again, telling Him that her bosom is as pure and her heart as inflamed as ever; tell Him that unless he comes into your soul, neither Jesus nor Mary will be formed nor find worthy lodging there.

3. After Holy Communion.

270. After Holy Communion, interiorly recollected and with eyes closed, you should introduce Jesus into the heart of Mary. Give Him to His Mother who will receive Him lovingly, set Him up in a place of honour, adore Him profoundly, love Him perfectly, closely embrace Him and in spirit and in truth will pay Him tokens of homage unknown to us in our deep darkness.[8]

271. Or else, you may remain profoundly humble in your heart, in the presence of Jesus living in Mary; or, like a slave, stand at the doors of the palace in which the King holds converse with His Queen, and whilst they speak together, without needing you, you will fly in spirit to Heaven and over the whole earth calling on all creatures to thank, adore and love Jesus in Mary for you: *Venite adoremus, venite.*[9]

272. Or again, you may ask Jesus yourself, in union with Mary, that His kingdom may come on earth through His Holy Mother; or you may ask for the gift of divine wisdom, for divine love, for the forgiveness of your sins, or some other grace, but always by Mary and in Mary; saying, while considering yourself disdainfully: *Ne respicias Domine peccata mea.*—"Lord, look not upon my sins";[10] *sed oculi tui videant*

---

7   "She is my greatest security, the whole reason of my hope." *De Aquaeductu.*
8   Cf. Prayer of St Gertrude: *O Maria, Virgo et Mater sanctissima.*
9   Ps. xciv, 6: "Come, let us adore."
10   Roman Missal: prayer before Communion.

aequitates Mariae.[11]—"Let Thine eyes behold nothing in me but the virtues and merits of Mary." Then, remembering your sins, you will add: *Inimicus homo hoc fecit*[12]—I myself, the greatest enemy I have to fight, have committed these sins; or else: *Ab homine iniquo et doloso erue me,*[13] or again: *Te oportet crescere, me autem minui.*[14] O Jesus, Thou must increase in my soul, and I must decrease. O Mary, thou must increase in me, and I must be less than I have been till now. *Crescite et multiplicamini:*[15] O Jesus and Mary, increase in me and in others around me.

273. There are many other thoughts which the Holy Ghost inspires and with which He will inspire you, if you are thoroughly recollected, mortified, and faithful to this great and sublime devotion that I have taught you. But remember that the more you let Mary act for you in your Communion, the more will Jesus be glorified. And the more deeply you humble yourself and listen to Jesus and Mary in peace and silence, without striving to see, taste or feel, the more you will let Mary act for Jesus and Jesus act in Mary; for the just man lives in all things by faith, and especially in receiving Holy Communion, which is an action of faith: *Justus meus ex fide vivit.*[16]

---

11   Ps. xvi, 2.
12   Mat. xiii, 28.
13   Ps. xlii, 1: "Deliver me from the unjust and deceitful man."
14   John iii, 30.
15   Gen. i, 28.
16   Heb. x, 38.

ACT OF CONSECRATION TO JESUS CHRIST, THE INCARNATE WISDOM, BY THE HANDS OF MARY.

O Eternal and Incarnate Wisdom! O sweetest and most adorable Jesus! True God and True Man, only Son of the Eternal Father and of Mary always Virgin! I adore Thee profoundly in the bosom and splendours of Thy Father during eternity, and in the virginal womb of Mary Thy most worthy Mother, in the time of Thy Incarnation.

I give Thee thanks that Thou hast emptied Thyself in taking the form of a slave in order to save me from the cruel slavery of the devil. I praise and glorify Thee that Thou hast been pleased to submit Thyself to Mary, Thy Holy Mother, in all things, in order to make me Thy faithful slave through her. But, alas! ungrateful and unfaithful as I have been, I have not kept the promises which I made so solemnly to Thee in my Baptism. I have not fulfilled my obligations; I do not deserve to be called Thy child nor yet Thy slave; and as there is nothing in me which does not merit Thine anger and repulse, I dare no longer come by myself before Thy most Holy and August Majesty. This is why I have recourse to the intercession of Thy Most Holy Mother, whom Thou hast given me to mediate with Thee. It is through her that I hope to obtain of Thee contrition and the pardon of my sins, the acquisition and the preservation of Wisdom.

Hail then, O Immaculate Mary, living Tabernacle of the Divinity, in which the Eternal Wisdom deigned to be hidden and to be adored by Angels and by men! Hail, O Queen of Heaven and earth to whose empire is subject everything that is under God! Hail, O sure Refuge of sinners, whose mercy fails no one! Grant the desire which I have to obtain the Divine

Wisdom, and for this end deign to accept the offering and promises which my lowliness presents to Thee.

I (N.N.), an unfaithful sinner, renew and ratify to-day in thy hands the promises of my Baptism: I renounce for ever Satan, his pomps and his works; and I give myself entirely to Jesus Christ, the Incarnate Wisdom, to carry my cross after Him all the days of my life and to be more faithful to Him than I have been till now.

I choose thee, this day, O Mary, in the presence of all the heavenly court, for my Mother and Mistress. I deliver and consecrate to thee, as thy slave, my body and soul, my goods, both interior and exterior, and even the value of my good actions past, present and future. I leave to thee the entire and full right to dispose of me and all that belongs to me, without exception, as thou pleasest, to the greater glory of God, in time and in eternity.

Receive, O gracious Virgin, this little offering of my slavery, in honour of and in union with that subjection which the Eternal Wisdom deigned to have to thy maternity, in homage to the power which both of you have over this little worm and miserable sinner, and in thanksgiving for the privileges with which the Holy Trinity has favoured thee. I protest that henceforth I wish, as thy true slave, to seek thy honour and to obey thee in all things.

O Admirable Mother, present me to thy dear Son as His eternal slave, so that as He has redeemed me by thee, by thee He may receive me! O Mother of Mercy, grant that I may obtain the true Wisdom of God, and for this end receive me among those whom thou lovest and teachest, whom thou leadest, nourishest and protectest as thy children and thy slaves.

O faithful Virgin, make me in all things so perfect a disciple, imitator and slave of the Incarnate Wisdom, Jesus Christ thy Son, that I may attain by thine intercession and example, to the fulness of His age on earth and of His glory in Heaven.

Amen.